D0815096

Iran's Developing Military Capabilities

Anthony H. Cordesman

THE CSIS PRESS

**Center for Strategic
and International Studies**

Washington, D.C.

Significant Issues Series, Volume 27, Number 4
© 2005 by Center for Strategic and International Studies
Washington, D.C.
All rights reserved
Printed on recycled paper in the United States of America
Cover design by Robert L. Wiser, Silver Spring, Md.
Cover photograph: Iranian soldiers march during a military parade in September
    2004. © Behrouz Mehri/ AFP / GettyImages.

09 08 07 06 05   5 4 3 2 1

ISSN 0736-7136
ISBN 0-89206-469-2

Library of Congress Cataloging-in-Publication Data
Cordesman, Anthony H.
    Iran's developing military capabilities / Anthony H. Cordesman.
        p. cm. — (Significant issues series; v. 27, no. 4)
    Includes bibliographical references.
    ISBN 0-89206-469-2
    1. Iran—Armed Forces. 2. Iran—Military policy. 3. Military planning—Iran. I.
Center for Strategic and International Studies (Washington, D.C.) II. Title. III. Series.
    UA853.I7C633 2005
    355'.033255—dc22

                                        2005009235

Iran's Developing Military Capabilities

Significant Issues Series
Timely books presenting current CSIS research and analysis of interest to the academic, business, government, and policy communities.
Managing Editor: Roberta L. Howard

The Center for Strategic and International Studies (CSIS) is a nonprofit, bipartisan public policy organization established in 1962 to provide strategic insights and practical policy solutions to decisionmakers concerned with global security. Over the years, it has grown to be one of the largest organizations of its kind, with a staff of some 200 employees, including more than 120 analysts working to address the changing dynamics of international security across the globe.

CSIS is organized around three broad program areas, which together enable it to offer truly integrated insights and solutions to the challenges of global security. First, CSIS addresses the new drivers of global security, with programs on the international financial and economic system, foreign assistance, energy security, technology, biotechnology, demographic change, the HIV/AIDS pandemic, and governance. Second, CSIS also possesses one of America's most comprehensive programs on U.S. and international security, proposing reforms to U.S. defense organization, policy, force structure, and its industrial and technology base and offering solutions to the challenges of proliferation, transnational terrorism, homeland security, and post-conflict reconstruction. Third, CSIS is the only institution of its kind with resident experts on all the world's major populated geographic regions.

CSIS was founded four decades ago by David M. Abshire and Admiral Arleigh Burke. Former U.S. senator Sam Nunn became chairman of the CSIS Board of Trustees in 1999, and since April 2000, John J. Hamre has led CSIS as president and chief executive officer.

Headquartered in downtown Washington, D.C., CSIS is a private, tax-exempt, 501(c) 3 institution.

The CSIS Press
Center for Strategic and International Studies
1800 K Street, N.W., Washington, D.C. 20006
Tel: (202) 887-0200 Fax: (202) 775-3199
E-mail: books@csis.org Web: www.csis.org

With assistance from Khalid Al-Rodhan and Patrick B. Baetjer

CONTENTS

LIST OF TABLES

LIST OF ABBREVIATIONS

AEOI	Atomic Energy Organization of Iran
APC	armored personnel carrier
BW	biological warfare
BWC	Biological Weapons Convention
CEP	circular area probable
CWC	Chemical Weapons Convention
EIA	U.S. Energy Information Administration
ENTC	Esfahan Nuclear Technology Centre
FEP	fuel enrichment plant
IAEA	International Atomic Energy Agency
IEA	International Energy Agency
IRGC	Islamic Revolutionary Guards Corps
LIS	laser isotope separation
MEK	Mujahideen-e Khalq
NPT	Nuclear Non-Proliferation Treaty
Pu	plutonium
TNRC	Tehran Nuclear Research Center
UCF	uranium conversion facility

INTRODUCTION

Iran is a nation with a mixed record in terms of Gulf and regional security. It no longer actively seeks to export its religious revolution to other Islamic states. It reached a rapprochement with Saudi Arabia and the other Southern Gulf states in the late 1990s. It has since avoided further efforts to try to use the Pilgrimage to attack the Kingdom, or to exploit Shi'ite versus Sunni tensions in Saudi Arabia and other Gulf countries like Bahrain. Iran maintains an active presence in the Gulf, conducts large scale-exercises, and maintains an active intelligence and surveillance presence in both the Gulf and neighboring states. It has avoided provocative military action, however, and there is no evidence of active hostile attacks on Southern Gulf targets or U.S. targets since the Al Khobar bombings.

Conversely, Iran no longer seems to be evolving toward a more moderate and democratic regime. It deals on at least low levels with outside terrorist groups. It actively supports the Hizballah in Lebanon and hard-line groups like Hamas and the Palestinian Islamic Jihad in attacking Israel. Iran is also well aware that Sunni and Shi'ite tensions are rising throughout the Islamic world, driven in part by Salafi extremist and terrorist groups like Al Qaeda.

Iran plays at least some role in the political instability in Iraq and may take a more aggressive role in trying to shape Iraq's political future and security position in the Gulf. Jordan's King Abdullah claimed that more than 1 million Iranians moved into Iraq to influence the Iraqi election. The Iranians, King Abdullah argued, have been trying to build pro-Iranian attitudes in Iraq by providing salaries to the unemployed. The king has also said that Iran's Revolutionary Guards are helping the militant groups fighting the United States in Iraq. He was quoted as saying "It's in Iran's vested interest to have an Islamic republic of Iraq."[1] The same sentiment has been echoed by the interim Iraqi president, Ghazi Al-Yawar: "Unfortunately. . . Iran has very obvious interference in our business [with] a lot of money, a lot of intelligence activities."[2]

Although such claims are far from verified, Iranian officials have at least hinted that any U.S. use of force against Iran could lead Iran to take action in Iraq. On December 3, 2004, Iran also conducted war games in the five western provinces, near the Iraqi border, involving 120,000 air and ground troops. A spokesperson for the Iranian army claimed that tanks, armored personnel carriers, fighters, and helicopters took part in the exercise.[3]

Iran is a far less modern military power in comparative terms than it was during the time of the shah or during the Iran-Iraq War. Nevertheless, it is slowly improving its conventional forces, and it is now the only regional military power that poses a serious conventional military threat to Gulf stability. Iran has significant capabilities for asymmetric warfare, and it poses the additional threat of proliferation. There is considerable evidence that it is developing both a long-range missile force and various weapons of mass destruction. It has never properly declared its holdings of chemical weapons, and the status of its biological weapons programs is unknown. The disclosures made by the International Atomic Energy Agency since 2002 indicate that Iran is likely to continue covertly seeking nuclear weapons.

Notes

[1] Robin Wright and Peter Baker, "Iraq, Jordan See Threat to Election from Iran," *Washington Post*, December 1, 2004.

[2] Ibid.

[3] Associated Press, "Iran Announces Largest War Games Exercise 'Ever' Near Iraq Borders," December 3, 2004.

CHAPTER ONE

IRANIAN CONVENTIONAL FORCES

Most of Iran's military equipment is aging or second rate, and much of it is worn. Iran lost some 50 to 60 percent of its land order of battle in the climactic battles of the Iran-Iraq War, and it has never had large-scale access to the modern weapons and military technology necessary to replace them. It also has lacked the ability to find a stable source of parts and supplies for most of its Western-supplied equipment, and it has not had access to upgrades and modernization programs since the fall of the shah in 1979.

IRANIAN MILITARY EXPENDITURES

Iran's military expenditures have been comparatively limited in recent years. The U.S. State Department provides declassified estimates for the period from 1989—the year after the Iran-Iraq War ended—to 1999. It estimates that military expenditures in current dollars ranged from $4,930 million to $8,260 million and declined slowly from average levels of $7,500 to $8,000 million in 1989–1990 to $7,000 million in 1999. This decline was much sharper in constant 1999 dollars. Iran was spending about $10 billion a year in 1989 and 1990, and its spending levels dropped to about $7,000 million in 1989–1990. According to the State Department estimates, military spending dropped from well in excess of 6 percent of Iran's gross national product in 1989 to less than 3 percent in 1999, and from 36 percent of all central government expenditures in 1989 to less than 12 percent in 1999. Iran's military spending from 1989 to 1999 is summarized in table 1.1.[1]

Table 1.1
Iran's Military Expenditures (ME) and Armed Forces (AF), 1989–1999

ME or AF	1989	1990	1991	1992	1993	1994	1995	1996	1997	1998	1999
ME current (million $)	7,690	8,260	7,930	5,090	6,060	6,030	4,930	5,240	6,620	7,050	6,880
ME constant (million $)	9,660	9,990	9,250	5,800	6,740	6,570	5,260	5,490	6,790	7,150	6,880
AF (thousands)	604	440	465	528	528	528	475	460	460	460	460
ME/CGE (%)	36.4	30.2	26.4	14.9	14.1	13.4	10.6	9.9	11.9	12.7	11.2
ME/GNP (%)	6.4	6.0	5.0	3.0	3.4	3.3	2.6	2.5	3.0	3.1	2.9
ME per capita constant	176	176	176	176	176	176	176	176	176	176	176

Source: Adapted by Anthony H. Cordesman from U.S. Department of State Bureau of Verification and Compliance, *World Military Expenditures and Arms Transfers 1999–2000* (Washington, D.C.: U.S. Department of State, various years).

Note: "Current" means in current dollars; "constant" means in 1999 dollars. "CGE" means central government expenditures.

The International Institute for Strategic Studies uses different definitions of military spending, and it indicates that Iran has an even lower level of effort. It estimates that spending was $4,000 million in 2000, $3,218 million in 2001, $3,077 million in 2002, and $3,051 in 2003. Expenditures did not increase with a major increase in Iran's oil export revenues during this period, and as a result, they dropped from 5.4 percent of Iran's gross domestic product (GDP) in 2000 to 2.4 percent in 2003. They have averaged only $46 to $50 per capita in recent years. To put these figures in perspective, the International Institute for Strategic Studies estimates that Saudi Arabia spent $21,055 million in 2001, $18,502 million in 2002, and $18,747 in 2003, ranging from 8.9 to 11.3 percent of its GDP. Its per capita military spending ranged from $832 to $984. [2]

IRANIAN ARMS IMPORTS

As table 1.2 shows, Iran is still dependent on large numbers of aging, worn, and obsolescent or obsolete weapons. Iran, however, was able to rebuild some of its conventional capabilities during the period 1988 to 2003, and it made progress toward acquiring weapons of mass destruction and long-range missiles.

As tables 1.3 and 1.4 show, Iran was able to make massive arms imports during the Iran-Iraq War and to obtain substantial supplies from the smaller European countries, China, and other communist suppliers. It was slow to understand the need to place massive orders, however, and many orders were only delivered toward the end of the war. Ironically, the end result was that when Iraq successfully counterattacked in 1988, it lost massive amounts of new equipment rushed onto the battlefield. These losses equaled some 40 to 60 percent of its total inventory of armor and significant amounts of its other land weapons inventory.

Iran also was unable to buy cutting-edge weapons from the former Soviet Union and to obtain significant amounts of modern arms from its suppliers at the time of the shah. Most of its deliveries during the period 1988–1992 were relatively low-grade weapons, although Russia did supply some modern armor and aircraft. Iran faced major financial problems until the mid-1990s and could not obtain resupply or new weapons from most Western states.

Table 1.2

Iranian Dependence on Decaying Western-supplied Major Weapons

Military Service and Weapon Type	Quantity	Comments
Land Forces		
Chieftain tank	100	Worn, underarmored, underarmed, and underpowered. Fire control and sighting system now obsolete. Cooling problems.
M-47/M-48	168	Worn, underarmored, underarmed, and underpowered. Fire control and sighting system now obsolete.
M-60A1	150–60	Worn, underarmored, underarmed, and underpowered. Fire control and sighting system now obsolete.
Scorpion AFV	80	Worn, light armor, underarmed, and underpowered.
M-114s	70	Worn, light armor, underarmed, and underpowered.
M-109 155 mm SP	180	Worn, fire control system now obsolete. Growing reliability problems due to lack of updates and parts.
M-107 175 mm SP	30	Worn, fire control system now obsolete. Growing reliability problems due to lack of parts.
M-110 203 mm SP	30	Worn, fire control system now obsolete. Growing reliability problems due to lack of parts.
AH-1J Attack Helicopters	50	Worn, avionics and weapons suite now obsolete. Growing reliability problems due to lack of updates and parts.
CH-47 Trans. Helicopters	20	Worn, avionics now obsolete. Growing reliability problems due to lack of updates and parts.

(continued next page)

(Table 1.2, continued)

Military Service and Weapon Type	Quantity	Comments
Bell, Hughes, Boeing, Augusta, Sikorsky Helicopters	145–85	Worn, growing reliability problems due to lack of updates and parts.
Air Force		
F-4D/E FGA	35–65	Worn, avionics now obsolete. Critical problems due to lack of updates and parts.
F-5E/F FGA	50–60	Worn, avionics now obsolete. Serious problems due to lack of updates and parts.
F-5/A/B	20–25	Worn, avionics now obsolete. Serious problems due to lack of updates and parts.
RF-4E	6	Worn, avionics now obsolete. Serious problems due to lack of updates and parts. (May be in storage.)
F-14 AWX	25	Worn, avionics now obsolete. Critical problems due to lack of updates and parts. Cannot operate some types of radar at long ranges. Phoenix missile capability cannot be used.
P-3F/ MPA	5	Worn, avionics and sensors now obsolete. Many sensors and weapons cannot be used. Critical problems due to lack of updates and parts.
Key PGMs	—	Remaining Mavericks, Aim-7s, Aim-9s, and Aim-54s are all long past rated shelf life. Many or most are unreliable or inoperable.
I-Hawk SAM	150	Worn, electronics, software, and some aspects of sensors now obsolete. Critical problems due to lack of updates and parts.

(continued next page)

(Table 1.2, continued)

Military Service and Weapon Type	Quantity	Comments
Rapier SAM	30	Worn, electronics, software, and some aspects of sensors now obsolete. Critical problems due to lack of updates and parts.
Tigercat SAM	15	Worn, electronics, software, and some aspects of sensors now obsolete. Critical problems due to lack of updates and parts.
Navy		
Alvand FFG	3	Worn, weapons and electronics suite obsolete, many systems inoperable or partly dysfunctional resulting from critical problems due to lack of updates and parts.
Bayandor FF	2	Obsolete. Critical problems due to lack of updates and parts.
Hengeman LST	4	Worn, needs full-scale refit.

Source: Estimate made by Anthony H. Cordesman based on the equipment counts in International Institute for Strategic Studies, The Military Balance (London: International Institute for Strategic Studies, various years) and discussions with U.S. experts. Note that different equipment estimates are used later in the text. The institute's figures are used throughout this table to preserve statistical consistency.

Iran did not carry out a major arms import effort once the Iran-Iraq War was over, and it received the backlog of arms imports from the orders it placed during the war. According to declassified U.S. intelligence estimates, Iran imported $8,800 million worth of arms from 1988 to 1991, but $3,000 million from 1992 to 1995, $2.0 billion from 1996 to 1999, and $600 million from 2000 to 2003. Iran signed $8,800 worth of new arms agreements from 1988 to 1991, but only $1,100 million from 1992 to 1995, $1,700 million from 1996 to 1999, and $500 million from 2000 to 2003. [3]

These trends are reinforced when one looks at the annual patterns in Iranian expenditures. As table 1.3 shows, the U.S. State Depart-

Table 1.3
Iran's Arms Imports, as Estimated by U.S. State Department, 1989–1999

Imports	1989	1990	1991	1992	1993	1994	1995	1996	1997	1998	1999
Arms imports current (million $)	19,00	1,900	1,600	850	1,400	390	360	370	900	370	150
Arms imports constant (million $)	23,89	2,300	1,869	969	1,559	425	384	388	925	376	150
Total arms imports / total imports (%)	14.8	9.3	5.7	3.3	6.5	2.8	2.6	2.3	4.4	2.7	0.9

Source: Adapted by Anthony H. Cordesman from U.S. Department of State Bureau of Verification and Compliance, *World Military Expenditures and Arms Transfers 1999–2000* (Washington, D.C.: U.S. Department of State, various years).

Note: "Current" means in current dollars; "constant" means in 1999 dollars.

Table 1.4
Congressional Research Service's Estimate of New Arms Agreements and Deliveries, 1980–2003
(current millions of dollars)

Agreement or Delivery and Period	United States	Russia	China	Major West European	All Other European	All Others	Total
New Agreements							
1980–1984*	0	240	505	1,520	1,675	1,355	5,295
1984–1987*	0	0	2,535	3,290	2,780	705	9,310
1988–1991	0	3,500	2,300	200	1,200	1,600	8,800
1992–1995	0	200	200	100	400	200	1,100
1996–1999	0	400	800	100	100	300	1,700
2000–2003	0	200	100	0	100	100	500
Deliveries							
1980–1984*	0	615	225	590	1,330	1,120	3,800
1984–1987*	**	5	1,590	2,995	2,565	775	7,930
1988–1991	0	1,600	3,100	300	1,400	1,500	7,900
1992–1995	0	1,700	700	100	200	300	3,000
1996–1999	0	900	700	100	300	0	2,000
2000–2003	0	200	0	0	0	400	600

Source: Based on the work of Richard F. Grimmett in Conventional Arms Transfers to Developing Nations (Washington, D.C.: Congressional Research Service, various years).

* Different categories are used for these years.

** No data on covert arms deliveries.

Note: 0 = Less than $50 million. All data have been rounded to the nearest $100 million. Russia = former Soviet Union. Major West European = France, Germany, Italy, and United Kingdom. All other European = all noncommunist European countries. All others = all other communist countries. Total is otherwise zero.

ment provides declassified estimates for the period from 1989—the year after the Iran-Iraq War ended—to 1999. It estimates that Iran's annual arms imports in current dollars ranged from $150 million to $1,900 million and declined slowly from average levels of $1,900 million in 1989–1990 to about $150 million in 1999. This decline was much sharper in constant 1999 dollars. Iran was spending around $2,300 to $2,400 million a year in 1989 and 1990, and its spending levels dropped to about $150–$400 million in 1989–1990.[4]

As table 1.5 shows, however, Iran has been able to gradually acquire significant numbers of capable and advanced weapons over time, particularly land-based and naval weapons. The following chapters also describe a number of areas where Iran has sought to produce or assemble its own weapons systems. These developments are summarized in table 1.6.

Nevertheless, Iran's current level of arms import and arms production is only about 35 to 50 percent of the level of imports necessary to recapitalize and modernize all of its forces. It also helps to explain why Iran lacks advanced new command, control, communications, computers, and intelligence systems and has not been able to modernize its air forces and ground-based air defenses or to develop major amphibious warfare capabilities. Iran is seeking to compensate in part through domestic military production, but its defense industry is not yet producing either the quality or quantity necessary to solve its problems.

OTHER PROBLEMS IN IRAN'S MILITARY MODERNIZATION

Iran's problems in military modernization have been compounded by a number of factors. The vast majority of the combat-trained labor power Iran developed during the Iran-Iraq War left military service by the mid-1990s. Iran now has a largely conscripted force with limited military training and little combat experience. The deep divisions between "moderates" and "hard-liners" in Iran's government inevitably politicized the armed forces, which remain under the command of the supreme religious leader, the Ayatollah Ali Khamenei. Iran retained divided armed forces, split between the regular forces that existed under the shah, and the Islamic Revolutionary Guards created under the Ayatollah Rhuholla Khomeini. This split was compounded

Table 1.5
Key Iranian Military Equipment Developments

Land

- Russian, and Polish T-72 Exports. Reports indicate Iran has procured about 380 T-72Ss from Russia (100 of which are kits for local assembly), and 100 T-72M1s from Poland since 1990. This gives Iran an inventory of about 480 T-72s—now its only truly modern tank and one where it has only taken delivery of 13 such tanks since 1995

- Claims to be producing the Iranian-made Zolfaqar (Zulfiqar) MBT, an M-48/M-60-like tank, but no more than 100 have been produced.

- Has upgraded to T-54/T-54 called "Safir-74. Claims to have upgraded Iraqi T-54s captured in Iran-Iraq War. Has 540 T-54/55 in inventory. Number of upgrades unknown.

- Purchased Russian BMPs. Inventory of 210 BMP-1s and 400 BMP-2s out a total of 865 armored infantry fighting vehicles and light tanks. .

- Russia may be licensing Iranian production of T-72 (100 units) and BMP-2 (200 units).

- Claims domestic production of a Chinese version of the BMP called the Boragh. May have an inventory of 140.

- Claims domestic production of an APC called the BMT-2 or Cobra.

- Possible purchase of 100 M-46 and 300 D-30 artillery weapons from Russia.

- Claims deployment of locally manufactured 122 mm and 155 mm self-propelled guns called Thunder-1 and Thunder-2, respectively. Some seem to be deployed but numbers are not available. Has 60 2S1 122 mm and 180 M-109 155 mm self-propelled weapon and some estimates indicate the Thunder-series weapons are with these units.

- May have 15+ Chinese and North Korean 146 mm self-propelled weapons.

- Has 60 Russian 2S1 122 mm self-propelled howitzers in inventory.

- Growing numbers of BM-24 240 mm, BM-21 122 mm, and Chinese Type 63 107 mm MRLs.

- Iranian Hadid 122 mm 50-round MRL.

- Manufacturing Iranian Arash and Noor rockets (variants of Chinese and Russian 122 mm rockets).

- Manufacturing Iranian Haseb rockets (variants of Chinese 107 mm rocket).

- Manufacturing Iranian Shahin 1 and 2, Oghab, Nazeat 5 and 10 (may be additional versions), and Fajr battlefield rockets.

- Has shown a modified heavy equipment transporter called the "Babr 400."

- Russian and Asian AT-2, AT-3, AT-4, and AT-5 antitank guided weapons. Reports of 100 Chinese Red Arrows seem incorrect.

(continued next page)

(Table 1.5, continued)

(Land, continued)

- Claims to have developed the Saeque-1 ATGW.
- Possible installation of a Russian T-72S main battle tank crew-training center.
- The Shebab-3 MRBM is assessed to enter its early operational status and it is estimated that Iran has some 20 missiles.
- Iran renewed its negotiation with Russia in early 2002 for large weapons deals. None, however, have materialized.

Air/Air Defense

- Keeping up to 115 combat aircraft that Iraq sent to Iran during Gulf War. Seem to include 24 Su-24s and four MiG-29s.
- Has 25 MiG-29s with air-to-air refueling capability in inventory. Reports may be receiving 15 to 20 more from Russia, but no confirmation.
- Has 30 Su-24s in inventory (Su-24MK). Reports may be receiving 6 to 9 more from Russia. But no confirmation.
- Has purchased AS-10, AS-11, AS-12, and AS-14/16s from Russia.
- Has 7 Su-25Ks (formerly Iraqi), although has not deployed.
- Reports may be trying to purchase more Su-25s, as well as MiG-31s, Su-27s, and Tu-22Ms.
- Considering imports of Chinese F-8 fighter and Jian Hong bomber.
- Has 24 Chinese F-7M fighters with PL2A, and PL-7 AAMs.
- Has purchased 15 Brazilian Tucano trainers and 22 Pakistani MiG-17 trainers.
- Has bought 12 Italian AB-212, 20 German BK-117A-3, and 2 Russian Mi-17 support and utility helicopters (30 Mi-17 to be delivered by the end of 2003).
- Iran claims to have fitted F-14s with I-Hawk missiles adapted to the air-to-air role.
- Claims to produce advanced electronic warfare systems.
- IRGC claims to be ready to mass-produce gliders.
- The first Iran-140 transport aircraft assembled under a joint program with Ukraine. Iran is planning to develop two versions of this aircraft for military use.
- The Iranian industry announced that it is planning to move the Azarakhsh combat aircraft and Shabaviz helicopters program into serial production.
- 20 Shahed-5 helicopter gunships in production. F-5 derived indigenous attack aircraft in development.

(continued next page)

(Table 1.5, continued)

Land-based Air Defense

- Most systems now aging or obsolescent in spite of some modifications.
- May be negotiating purchase of S-300 and more SA-14/16s from Russia.
- Has acquired four HQ-23/2B (CSA-1) launchers and 45 to 48 missiles, plus 25 SA-6 and 10 SA-5 launchers.
- Has acquired Chinese FM-80 launchers and a few RBS-70s.
- More SA-7s and HN-5s man-portable missiles; may have acquired 100 to 200 Strelas.
- Reports is seeking to modernize Rapier and 10 to 15 Tigercat fire units.
- May be modifying and/or producing ZSU-23-4 radar-guided antiaircraft guns.
- Claims to produce advanced electronic warfare systems.

Sea

- Claims will soon start producing 3 corvettes.
- Has taken delivery on three Russian Type 877EKM Kilo-class submarines, possibly with 1,000 modern magnetic, acoustic, and pressure sensitive mines.
- Reports of North Korean midget submarines have never been confirmed. Has produced small swimmer delivery vehicles called the Al-Sabehat 15 minisubmarine.
- Main surface ships are 3 Alvan (Vosper 5)–class frigates dating back to late 1960s and early 1970s, and two Bayandor-class frigates from early 1980s.
- Obtained 10 Hudong-class Chinese missile patrol boats with CS-802 during early to middle 1990s. Has 10 Kaman-class missile patrol boats from late 1970s and early 1980s.
- U.S. Mark 65 and Russian AND 500, AMAG-1, and KRAB antiship mines.
- Reported that Iran is negotiating to buy Chinese EM-52 rocket-propelled mine.
- Iran claims to be developing nonmagnetic, acoustic, free-floating, and remote-controlled mines. It may have also acquired nonmagnetic mines, influence mines, and mines with sophisticated timing devices.
- Wake-homing and wire-guided Russian torpedoes.
- Seersucker (HY-2) sites with 50–60 missiles—Iran working to extend range to 400 km.
- Has 60 to 100 Chinese CS-801(Ying Jai-1 SY-2) and CS-802 (YF-6) SSMs.
- Iran is developing FL-10 antiship cruise missile that is copy of Chinese FL-2 or FL-7.

(continued next page)

(Table 1.5, continued)

(Sea, continued)

- Boghammer fast interceptor craft.
- The Iranian navy received fast patrol boats and C-701 shipborne missiles from China.
- Iran received 15 small patrol boats from North Korea.

Missiles

- Obtained up to 300 Scud Bs with 12 to 18 launchers.
- Some 175 Chinese CSS-8 surface-to-surface missiles with 25 to 30 launchers.
- Reports that China is giving Iran technology to produce long-range solid-fuel missiles.
- Mushak-90, -120, -160, and -200 missiles based on the Chinese CSS-8.
- Has bought North Korean Scud Cs with 5 to 14 launchers. South Korea reports Iran has bought total of 100 Scud Bs and 100 Scud Cs from North Korea.
- May be developing the Zelzal-3 missile with a range of 900 km with Chinese and North Korean support.
- Iran has tested the Shahab-3 (which may have a 1,500 km range and is based on the North Korean No-dong 1) and may have started production.
- Iran may be planning to purchase North Korean No-Dong 1/2s.
- Has shown interest in technology for interested in North Korea's developmental Tapeo Dong 1 or Tapeo Dong 2.
- Reports of tunnels for hardened deployment of Scuds and SAMs.
- Possible deployment of locally produced Nazeat series missiles, based on Russian FROG missiles.

Chemical and Biological Weapons

- Chemical weapons (sulfur mustard gas, hydrogen cyanide, phosgene, and/or chlorine; possibly Sarin and Tabun).
- Biological weapons (possibly Anthrax, hoof and mouth disease, and other biotoxins).
- Nuclear weapons development (Russian and Chinese reactors).

Sources: Based on interviews; reporting in various defense journals; *Jane's Fighting Ships*; International Institute for Strategic Studies, *The Military Balance* (Oxford: International Institute for Strategic Studies, various years); and Jaffee Center for Strategic Studies, *The Middle East Military Balance* (Tel Aviv: Jaffee Center for Strategic Studies, various years).

Table 1.6
Can Iran Mass-produce Major New Weapons Systems?

Land

- Can produce nearly 50 types of munitions, including tank rounds, artillery shells, and rockets. Probably meets between 50 and 75 percent of Iran's needs in a major regional contingency, and their output is steadily building up Iran's reserves.

- Manufacturers most of Iran's assault rifles, mortars up though 120 mm in caliber, and antitank rocket launchers.

- Showed prototype of a main battle tank called the Zulfiqar (Zolfaqar) in 1994. Tank has undergone field trials ever since the Velayat military exercises of May 1996. Its drive train and suspension seem to be modeled on the U.S.-designed M-48A5 and M-60A1 series of tanks and to have either a 105 mm or 125 mm rifled gun. Reports differ as to the Zulfiqar's production status. One report indicates that Iran announced on July 8, 1997, that President Rafsanjani opened the "first phase" of a plant to produce the tank in Dorud, some 300 kilometers southwest of Tehran. Another report indicates that it is produced at the Shahdid Industrial Complex. Up to 100 may have been produced.

- T-72S (Shilden) tanks being assembled under license.

- Upgrading T-54s, T-55s, and T-59s with 105 mm gun made in Iran and new fire control system.

- Claims ready to produce light tank for "unconventional warfare" called the Towan (Wild Horse) with 90 mm gun.

- Developed Iranian-made modification of the Chinese Type WZ 501/503 armored infantry fighting vehicle that Iran calls the Boragh. The WZ 501/503 is itself a Chinese copy of the Russian BMP, and is 30-year-old technology. Up to 120 may be in inventory.

- Displayed APC called the Cobra or BMT-2, which seems to be an indigenous design armed with a 30 mm gun or the ZU-23-2 antiaircraft gun—a light automatic weapons system that Iran has been manufacturing for some years. Like the Zulfiqar, the Cobra has been undergoing field trials in Iranian military exercises since May 1996.

- Iran now makes a number of antitank weapons. These include an improved version of the man-portable RPG-7 antitank rocket with an 80 mm tandem HEAT warhead instead of the standard 30 mm design, the NAFEZ antitank rocket, and a copy of the Soviet SPG-9 73 mm recoilless antitank gun. Iran also makes a copy of the Russian AT-3 9M14M (Sagger or Ra'ad) antitank guided missile.

- Claimed in May 1996 to have produced a self-propelled version of a Russian 122 mm gun that it called the Thunder-1, with a firing range of 15,200 meters and a road speed of 65 kilometers per hour.[a] It may use the Boragh chassis for this weapon. It also claimed to have tested a "rapid fire" 155 mm self-propelled weapon in September 1997 called the Thunder 2. Some seem to have been deployed.

(continued next page)

(Table 1.6, continued)

(Land, continued)

- Makes military radios and low-technology remotely piloted vehicles, like the 22006, Baz, and Shahin.

- Has developed tactical radios ART 2000, VHF frequency-hopping radio with a range of 30–88 MHz, and the PRC-110 HF fixed-frequency man-pack radio, which covers the 1.6–29.999 H MHz band in 100 Hz steps. (*Jane's International Defense Review*, June 1998, 22.)

- Has developed low-drag 155mm high-explosive base-bleed projectile. The 155BB HE-TNT incorporates a 16 kg TNT and has a range of 35 km when fired with an M11 top charge from a 45-caliber gun. Range is 17 km without base bleed. A new low-drag, high-explosive projectile for 120 mm smoothbore mortars with a range of 13.2 km. (*Jane's International Defense Review*, June 1998, 22.)

Air/Air Defense

- Necessary technical sophistication to rebuild the jet engines for many of its American fighters and helicopters.

- Produce parts and modifications for some of its types of radar, missile systems, avionics, ships, and armored personnel carriers.

- Claims to have built its first Iranian-designed helicopter, and to have tested a locally built fighter plane. Brigadier General Arasteh, a deputy head of the General Staff of the Armed Forces (serving under Major General Ali Shahbazi, the joint chief of staff) stated in April 1997 that the "production line of this aircraft will begin work in the near future."

- Chinese F-7 assembled in Iran.

- Defense Industries Organization claimed that Iran was soon going to start producing two trainers, a jet-powered Dorna (Lark) and propeller-driven Partsu (Swallow).

- There had been reports in 1996 that Iran had obtained Ukrainian aid in producing the Antonov An-140 at a factory in Esfahan. In September 1997, Iran indicated that it had signed a contract to buy 10 Antonov An-74 transport jets, and reports surfaced that it might coproduce the An-T74T-200. In November 1998, it was reported that the first of the 52-seat An-140 will roll off the assembly line next year. (*Jane's Defence Weekly*, November 4, 1998.)

- Iran has upgraded some of its F-4s, F-14s, and C-130s.

- Iranian military claimed that Iran has begun mass production of a jet strike aircraft, the Azarakhsh (Lightning), which reportedly resembles the F-4 Phantom. (*Jane's Defence Weekly*, November 4, 1998.)

- Iranian Air Force claims that it is developing two combat aircraft based on the F-5 and a third indigenously designed. (*Jane's Defence Weekly*, November 20, 2002.)

(continued next page)

(Table 1.6, continued)

(Air/Air Defense, continued)

- Armed Forces Air Industries Organization was discussing, in November 1998, a deal with Ukraine's Aviant Aviatsiny Zavod, coproducer of the new Tupolev-334, to build the planes in Iran. The deal would be for the production of 100 of the 100-seat aircraft over 15 years. (*Jane's Defense Weekly*, November 4, 1998; Reuters, October 12, 1998.)
- Iran has reportedly developed a TV-guided missile for carriage on F-4 Phantoms.
- Iran claims to have deployed an air-to-air adapted variant of the SM1 Standard missile for its fleet of F-4D/E Phantom II fighter-bombers. (*Jane's Defence Weekly*, April 29, 1998.)

Land-based Air Defense

- President Hashemi Rafsanjani announced on October 11, 1997, that Iran had test-launched a major new surface-to-air missile system with a range of 250 km, although he gave no further details. The description of the missile sounded vaguely like the Russian SA-5, which is deployed in Iran. Reports has acquired four HQ-23/2B (CSA-1) launchers and 45 to 48 missiles, plus 25 SA-6 and 10 to 15 SA-5 launchers.
- May be modifying and/or producing ZSU-23-4 radar-guided antiaircraft guns.
- Claims to produce advanced electronic warfare systems.

Sea

- Claims will soon start producing 6 multipurpose destroyers, with initial production run of three.
- Constructing small submarine?
- Iran claims to be developing nonmagnetic, acoustic, free-floating, and remote-controlled mines. It may have also acquired nonmagnetic mines, influence mines, and mines with sophisticated timing devices.
- Wake-homing and wire-guided Russian torpedoes.
- Iran is developing FL-10 antiship cruise missile that is copy of Chinese FL-2 or FL-7.
- Reportedly assembled domestic variants the YJ-1 (C-801) solid-propellant antiship missile under the local name of Karus, and the YJ-2 (C-802) turbojet-powered antiship missile under the local name of Tondar. (*Jane's Defence Weekly*, December 9, 1998.)
- Boghammer fast interceptor craft.

Missiles

- Iranian made IRAN 130 rocket with 150+ km range.
- Iranian Oghab (Eagle) rocket with 40+ km range.

(continued next page)

(Table 1.6, continued)

(Missiles, continued)

- New SSM with 125 mile range may be in production but could be modified FROG.

- Developing the Zelzal-3 missile with a range of 900 km with Chinese and North Korean support.

- Claims that Russia is helping Iran develop four missiles. These missiles include:

   Shahab 3—a liquid-fueled missile with a range of 810 miles (1,200–1,500 km) and a payload of 1,550 pounds, based on North Korean Nodong missile. Israel claims the Shahab might be ready for deployment as early as 1999.

   Shahab 4, with a range of 1,250 miles (1,995 km) and a payload in excess of 1 ton, based on the Russian R-12, may be in service in 2001. However, the Ministry of Defense released a statement declaring that Iran had no intention of building the Shahab 4 and would continue to rely on the Shahab 3 and potential future variants.[b]

   Other two missiles are longer-range systems with a maximum ranges of 4,500 and 10,000 km.

- Iran is reportedly receiving or trying to receive steel from China and Russia for the production of missiles.

- Has tested Iranian made Fajr-4 ballistic missiles and new version of Fajr-3 missile, with a range of 28 miles (45 km).

- Has developed solid-propellant surface-to-surface missiles: the Zelzal 2, Nazeat and Shahin.

- Reports of tunnels for hardened deployment of Scuds and SAMs.

- Experimenting with cruise missile development, although no links as yet to the employment of such missiles with warheads using weapons of mass destruction.

Chemical and Biological Weapons

- Chemical weapons (sulfur mustard gas, hydrogen cyanide, phosgene, and/ or chlorine; possibly Sarin and Tabun).

- Biological weapons (possibly Anthrax, hoof and mouth disease, and other biotoxins).

- Nuclear weapons development (Russian and Chinese reactors).

Sources: Based on interviews, reporting in various defense journals; and International Institute for Strategic Studies, *The Military Balance* (London: International Institute for Strategic Studies, various years).

[a]*Jane's Defence Weekly*, June 5, 1996.

[b]Robin Hughes, "Iran Denies Shahab 4 Development," *Jane's Defence Weekly*, November 12, 2003.

by a highly bureaucratic and "stovepiped" command structure, which made limited progress in joint warfare.

Nevertheless, Iran is still a significant conventional military power by Gulf standards. It has some 540,000 men under arms, and more than 350,000 reserves. These include 120,000 members of the Islamic Revolutionary Guards Corps trained for land and naval asymmetric warfare. Iran's military also includes holdings of 1,613 main battle tanks, 1,500 other armored fighting vehicles, 3,200 artillery weapons, 306 combat aircraft, 50 attack helicopters, 3 submarines, 59 surface combatants, and 10 amphibious ships.

Notes

[1] U.S. State Department, *World Military Expenditures and Arms Transfers, 1999–2000* (Washington, D.C.: U.S. Government Printing Office, 2000), 77.

[2] The counts of Iran's military labor power, weapons numbers and types, force strength, and defense expenditures in this book rely heavily on various editions of International Institute for Strategic Studies, *The Military Balance* (London: International Institute for Strategic Studies, various years). These figures are taken from *The Military Balance, 2004–2005,* 354–355.

[3] Richard F. Grimmett, *Conventional Arms Transfer to Developing Nations, 1996–2000* (Washington, D.C.: Congressional Research Service, 2004), 50, 61.

[4] U.S. State Department, *World Military Expenditures and Arms Transfers,* 77.

CHAPTER TWO

THE IRANIAN ARMY

The Iranian Army is large by regional standards. It has some 350,000 men (220,000 conscripts) organized into four corps, with four armored divisions, six infantry divisions, two commando divisions, an airborne division, and other smaller independent formations. These latter units include independent armored, infantry, and commando brigades' six artillery groups, and army aviation units.

In practice, each Iranian division has a somewhat different organization. For example, only one Iranian division (the 92nd) is equipped well enough in practice to be a true armored division, and two of the armored divisions are notably larger than the others. Two of the infantry divisions (the 28th and 84th) are more heavily mechanized than the others.[1] The lighter and smaller formations in the regular army include the 23rd Special Forces Division, which was formed in 1993–1994, and the 55th Paratroop Division. According to one source, the 23rd Special Forces Division has 5,000 full-time regulars and is one of the most professional units in the Iranian Army.

The airborne and special forces are trained at a facility in Shiraz.[2] The regular army also has a number of independent brigades and groups. These include some small armored units, 1 infantry brigade, 1 airborne, and 2 to 3 special forces brigades, coastal defense units, a growing number of air defense groups, 5 artillery brigades and regiments, 4 to 6 army aviation units, and a growing number of logistic and supply formations. The land forces have 6 major garrisons and 13 major casernes. There are a military academy at Tehran and a signal-training center in Shiraz.[3]

Table 2.1 provides the details of the development of the force structure in the Iranian army since the end of its war with Iraq in 1989, levels of labor power, and numbers and types of major weapons.

IRANIAN TANK STRENGTH

Iran has steadily rebuilt its armored strength since the Iran-Iraq War. It has some 1,613 main battle tanks, and the number has risen steadily in recent years. Iran had a total of 1,135 in 2000 and 1,565 in 2003. The International Institute for Strategic Studies estimates that Iran's inventory of main battle tanks now includes some 150 M-47/M-48s and 150 to 160 M-60A1s, 100 Chieftain Mark 3/5s, 250 T-54/T-55s, 150 to 250 T-59s, 75 T-62s, 480 T-72/T-72S, and 100 Zulfiqars. Its T-72 strength has increased from 120 in 2000. (Other estimates indicate that Iran may have as many as 300 Type 59s and/or 150 to 250 T-69IIs.)

Only part of Iran's tank inventory is fully operational. It is uncertain how many Chieftains and M-47/M-48s are really operational, although its Chieftains include the remainder of 187 improved FV4030/1 versions of the Mark 5 Chieftain that were delivered to Iran before the fall of the shah. Smaller problems seem to exist in the rest of the force, and some experts estimate that Iran's sustainable *operational* tank strength may be fewer than 1,000 tanks. Furthermore, Iran's Chieftains and M-60s are at least 16 to 20 years old, and the T-72 and Zulfiqar are Iran's only tanks with advanced fire control systems, sights, and armor-piercing ammunition.

Iran's T-72Ss are export versions of the Soviet T-72B. Some have been built under license in Iran and are armed with a 125 millimeter (mm) 2A46M smoothbore gun. They have a relatively modern IA40-1 fire control system and computer, a laser range finder, and a night-and-day image-intensifying sighting system. The T-72S is powered by an 840 horsepower V-84MS diesel engine, has an upgraded suspension and mine protection, and has a combat weight of 44.5 tons. Russian sources indicate that Iran has ordered a total of 1,000 T-72s from Russia.

Iran has developed a main battle tank called the Zulfiqar, with a 125 mm smoothbore gun and welded steel turret of Iranian design. According to one report, the Zulfiqar is powered by a V-46-6-12 V-12

Table 2.1
Iran's Army: Force Structure Trends, 1989–2005

Aspect of Force Structure	1989–1990	1999–2000	2004–2005
Labor power	305,000	350,000	350,000
Active	305,000	350,000	350,000
Conscripts	250,000	220,000	220,000
Combat units			
Army HQ	3	4	4
Armored Division	0	4	4
Mechanize Brigade	0	1	1
Artillery Battalion	0	4–5	4–5
Infantry Division	6	6	6
Artillery Battalion	?	4–5	4–5
Commando Division	0	1	2
Airborne Division	1	1	1
Special Operation Division	1	1	?
Mechanized Division	4	0	0
Mechanized Battalion	28	0	0
Armored Brigade	9	0	0
Main battle tanks	500	1,345	1,613
T-54	?	400	540
T-59	?	0	0
T-62	?	75	75
T-72	?	480	480
Chieftain Mk 3/5	?	140	100
M-47/-48	?	150	168
M-60A1	?	100	150
Zulfiqar	0	0	100
Light tanks	30	80	80+
Scorpion	30	80	80
Towsan	0	0	?
RECCE	130	35	35
EE-9 Cascavel	130	35	35
AIFV	**100+**	440	610
BMP-1	100+	300	210
BMP-2	0	140	400

(continued next page)

(Table 2.1, continued)

Aspect of Force Structure	1989–1990	1999–2000	2004–2005
APC	500	550	640
BTR-50/-60	?	300	300
M-113	?	250	200
Boragh	0	0	140
Towed	?	2,170	2,095
105 mm: M-101A1	339+	130	130
105 mm: Oto Melara	36	0	0
122 mm: D-30	0	600	540
122 mm: PRC type-54	0	100	100
130 mm: M-46/Type-59	125	1,100	985
152 mm: D-20	0	30	30
155 mm: WAC-21	0	20	100
155 mm: M-114	0	70	70
155 mm: FH-77B	18	0	0
155 mm: GHN-45	130	100	120
203 mm: M-115	30	20	20
Self-propelled	140	290	310+
122 mm: 2S1	0	60	60
122 mm: Thunder 1	0	0	?
155 mm: M-109	100	60	180
155 mm: Thunder 2	0	0	?
170 mm: M-1978	0	10	10
175 mm: M-107	30	30	30
203 mm: M-110	10	30	30
Multiple rocket launchers		764+	860+
107 mm: PRC Type-63	?	600	700
107 mm: Haseb	0	0	?
107 mm: Fadjr 1	0	0	?
122 mm: Hadid/Arash/Noor	0	50	50
122 mm: BM-21	65	100	100
122 mm: BM-11	?	5	7
240 mm: M-1985	0	9	9
240 mm: Fadjr 3	0	0	10
333 mm: Fadjr 5	0	0	?

(continued next page)

(Table 2.1, continued)

Aspect of Force Structure	1989–1990	1999–2000	2004–2005
Mortars	3,000+	6,500	5,000
60 mm	0	?	?
81 mm	?	?	?
82 mm	0	?	?
107 mm: 4.2 in. M-30	?	?	?
120 mm: M-65	3,000	?	?
Surface-to-surface missiles		?	?
Scud-B/-C Launchers/Launch Vehicles	?	10	12–18
Shahab 3	?	?	?
CSS-8	0	25	30
Oghab	?	?	?
Shahin 1/-2	?	?	?
Nazeat	?	?	?
ATGW	?	?	75
ENTAC	?	0	0
SS-11/-12	?	0	0
Dragon	?	0	0
AT-3 Sagger	0	0	?
AT-4 Spigot	0	?	?
AT-5 Spandrel	0	0	?
Saeqhe 1/2	0	0	?
Toophan	0	0	?
Rocket launchers	0	?	?
73 mm: RPG-7	0	?	?
Recoilless launchers	?	?	?
57 mm	?	0	0
75 mm: M-20	?	?	?
82 mm: B-10	0	?	?
106 mm: M-40	?	?	200
107 mm: B-11	0	?	?
Air defense guns	1,500	1,700	1,700
14.5 mm: ZPU-2/-4	?	?	?
23 mm: ZU-23 Towed	?	?	?
23 mm: ZSU-23-4 SP	?	?	?
35 mm:?	?	?	?

(continued next page)

(Table 2.1, continued)

Aspect of Force Structure	1989–1990	1999–2000	2004–2005
(Air defense guns, continued)			
37 mm: M-1939	?	?	?
37 mm: PRC Type-55	?	?	?
57 mm: ZSU-57-2-Sp	?	?	?
57 mm: S-60	?	?	?
Surface-to-air missiles	230	?	?
I Hawk	30	0	0
RBS-70	200	?	?
SA-7/-14/-16	?	?	?
HQ-7	0	?	?
UAV	0	?	?
Mohajer II/III/IV	0	?	?
Aircraft	49+	77	36
Cessna 185	40+	50	10
F-27	2	19	2
Falcon 20	2	8	20
Turbo Commander 690	5	0	4
Helicopters	410	556	223
AH-1J Attack	100	100	50
CH-47C Heavy Transport	10	40	20
Bell 214A/C	250	165	50
Bell 204	0	30	0
AB-205A	35	40	68
AB-206	15	90	10
AB-12	0	12	0
Mi-8/-17	0	0	25
Hughes 300C	0	5	0
RH-53D	0	9	0
SH-53D	0	10	0
SA-319	0	10	0
UH-1H	0	45	0

Source: Adapted by Anthony H. Cordesman from International Institute for Strategic Studies, *The Military Balance* (London: International Institute for Strategic Studies, various years).

Note: (1) The equipment includes that of the Islamic Revolutionary Guards Corps. (2) A "?" means that the International Institute for Strategic Studies does not report the exact number, and a "+" means that number or greater.

diesel engine with 780 horsepower and uses a SPAT 1200 automatic transmission. This engine is used in the Soviet T-72, but the tank transmission design seems to be closer to that of the U.S. M-60. It seems to have a relatively modern fire control system, and Iran may have improved its T-72s with a similar upgrade. The Zulfiqar's combat weight is reported to be 36 tons, and it is said to have a maximum speed of 65 kilometers (km) per hour and a power-to-weight ratio of 21.7 horsepower per ton. It has a 7.62 mm coaxial and a 12.7 mm roof-mounted machine gun.[4]

According to some reports, it uses the Fontana (EFCS)-3-72 Enhanced Fire Control System. Slovenian analysts indicate, however, that the system was exported to Iran via Austria in the mid-1990s and was intercepted by Austrian customs. There is the possibility that it was later exported via a third party to Iran or that the former Yugoslavia exported some parts of the former Yugoslav MBT M-84 fire control system called SUV-84, which is very similar, at least in outside appearance, to the EFCS-3-72 and is produced by factory called Rudi Cajevec that originally was in Bosnia but was evacuated to Serbia at the beginning of the 1990s.

It uses modern Slovenia Fontana EFCS-3 computerized fire control system to provide a fully stabilized fire on the move capability. It may have a roof-mounted laser warning device, and it could use the same reactive armor system discussed above. Roughly 100 Zulifqars seem to be in service.

Iran has extended the life of some of its T-54s, T-55s, and T-59s by improving their armor and fire control systems, and by arming them with an Iranian-made M-68 rifled 105 mm gun similar to the one used on the M-60A1. This weapon seems to be made by the Armament Industries Division of the Iranian Defense Industries Organization. The Islamic Revolutionary Guards Corps (IRGC) is reported to have a special conversion of the T-54 called the Safir-74. Iran has developed explosive reactive armor add-ons for its tanks, although the effectiveness of such armor and the extent of such uparmoring of any given model of tank is unclear.

Iran's 168 M-47/M-48s include Iran's surviving upgraded M-47Ms. These M-47s were upgraded by the American firm of Bowen-McLaughlin York between 1970 and 1972, which also built a vehicle-manufacturing plant in Iran. They have many of the components of the M-60A1, including the diesel engine, automatic transmission, suspension, and gun control and fire components. The conversion extended the operating range of the M-47 from 130 to 600 km, and it increased space to hold 79 rounds by eliminating the bow-mounted machine gun and reducing the crew to four. A total of about 150 conversions seem to have been delivered to Iran.

In spite of its tank deliveries and production since the Iran-Iraq War, Iran's total operational main battle tank holdings are only sufficient to fully equip five to seven of its divisions by Western standards, and Iran could only sustain about half this force for any period of extended maneuver warfare. At present, however, they are dispersed in relatively small lots among all its regular Army and some of its IRGC combat units—all the IRGC units generally only have small tank force cadres, and it is unclear how heavy these forces will really be in the future. The 92nd Armored Division is the only Iranian division that has enough tanks to be a true armored division, even by regional standards.

OTHER IRANIAN ARMOR

Iran seems to have about 1,000 to 1,360 armored infantry fighting vehicles (AFVs) and armored personnel carriers (APCs) in its operational inventory, although counts are contradictory and it is difficult to estimate what parts of Iran's holdings are fully operational and/or sustainable for any length of time in combat. The International Institute for Strategic Studies, for example, estimates 80 light tanks, 610 armored infantry fighting vehicles, and 640 APCs. Virtually all estimates indicate, however, that Iran only has about half the total holdings that it would need to fully mechanize its forces.[5] This total compares with about 3,000 to 3,600 such weapons for Saudi Arabia.

Iran has 865 other AFVs, of which 650 are active, including 210 BMP-1s and 400 BMP-2s. This compares with a total of 555 such weapons in 2000, which then included only 140 BMP-2s. Iran appears to retain 70 to 80 British-supplied Scorpions out of the 250 it received before the fall of the shah. These are tracked weapons equipped with 76 mm guns. However, the Scorpion is more than 20 years old, and as few as 30 may be fully operational. These problems may explain why Iran has developed a new light tank called the Tosan (Towsan, "Wild

Horse," or "Fury") with a 90 mm gun, some of which may now be in service.[6]

Iran has some 210 BMP-1s and 400 BMP-2 equivalents in service (some estimates say 350 BMP-1s and 400 BMP-2s). The BMPs are Soviet-designed systems, but the BMP-1s in particular have serious ergonomic and weapons suite problems. They are hard to fight from, hard to exit, and too slow to keep pace with modern tanks. They lack thermal vision systems and modern long-range fire control systems, and their main weapons are hard to operate in combat, even from static positions. Nevertheless, many have smoothbore antitank guns and antitank guided missiles. Iran also has at least 35 EE-9 Cascavel armored reconnaissance vehicles, and one estimate indicates 100. The Cascavel is an acceptable design for combat in the developing world, although it lacks modern sensors and weapons.

Iran is much less well equipped to provide its forces with adequate armored mobility. It has 550 to 670 APCs. No more than 600 are operational, and most are worn and aging BTR-50s and BTR-60s (300–320), or M-113s (230–50) that are more than a quarter of a century old and have not be updated.

Iran is producing an armored fighting vehicle called the Boragh (Boraq) and a lighter APC called the Cobra or BMT-2, and some 40 to 120 are in service—depending on the source of the report. There are different views over whether such weapons should be classed as AFVs or APCs. The Boragh seems to be a copy of a Chinese version of the BMP-1. It is a fully tracked and amphibious and has a combat weight of 13 tons. It can carry 8 to 12 people, plus two crew. Reports differ as to its armament—perhaps reflecting different variants. Initial reports indicated that it has a turret armed with a 73 mm smoothbore gun and antitank guided missile launcher. It may, however, lack the commander's position that exists in the BMP-1 and be armed with a 12.7 mm machine gun. Iran has developed an armor package designed to fit over the hull of the Boragh to provide protection against 30 mm armor-piercing ammunition.[7] Variants with 120 mm mortars, one-man turrets with Iranian-made Toophan ATGMs and AT-4 ATGMs, and others with 73 mm BMP-2 turret guns also seem to be deploying.

The Cobra or BMT-2 is clearly an APC. It is a low-profile, wheeled troop carrier, which can hold seven personnel. Some versions may have twin 23 mm AA guns.

Iran has an unknown number of British Chieftain bridging tanks, a wide range of specialized armored vehicles, and some heavy equipment transporters. Iran is steadily improving its ability to support armored operations in the field and to provide recovery and field repair capability. However, its exercises reveal that these capabilities are still limited relative to those of U.S. forces and that a lack of recovery and field repair capability, coupled with poor interoperability, will probably seriously limit the cohesion, speed, and sustainability of Iranian armored operations.

Iran's armored warfare doctrine seems to be borrowed from U.S., British, and Russian sources without achieving any coherent concept of operations. Even so, Iran's armored doctrine is improving more quickly than its organization and exercise performance. Iran's armored forces are very poorly structured, and Iran's equipment pool is spread between far too many regular and IRGC units. Iran has only one armored division—the 92nd Armored Division—with enough tanks and other armor to be considered a true armored unit.

IRANIAN ANTITANK WEAPONS

Iran has large holdings of antitank guided weapons and has been manufacturing copies of Soviet systems while buying missiles from China, Russia, and Ukraine. It has approximately 50 to 75 TOW and 20 to 30 Dragon antitank guided missile launchers that were originally supplied by the United States, although the operational status of such systems is uncertain. It has Soviet and Asian versions of the AT-2, AT-3, AT-4, and AT-5. Iran seems to have at least 100 to 200 AT-4 (9K111) launchers, but it is impossible to make an accurate estimate because Iran is producing its own copies of the AT series called the Towsan. According to some reports, it is also making copies of the Dragon (Saeqhe) and TOW (Toophan).

Iran has some 750 RPG-7V, RPG-11, and 3.5 inch rocket launchers, and roughly 150 M-18 57 mm, 200 M-20 75 mm and B-10 82 mm, and 200 M-40 106 mm and B-11 107 mm recoilless guns.

Iran makes a number of antitank weapons. These include an improved version of the man-portable RPG-7 antitank rocket with an 80 mm tandem HEAT warhead instead of the standard 30 mm design, the NAFEZ antitank rocket, and a copy of the Soviet SPG-9 73 mm recoilless antitank gun. Iran also makes a copy of the Russian AT-3 9M14M (Sagger or Ra'ad) antitank guided missile. This system is a crew-operable system with a guidance system that can be linked to a launcher holding up to four missiles. It has a maximum range of 3,000 meters, a minimum range of 500 meters, and a flight speed of 120 meters per second. Iran is also seeking more advanced technology from Russian arms firms, and some reports indicate that it may be able to make copies of the AT-4 and/or AT-5. The United States maintains that a firm sold Iran Krasnopol artillery shells, but the company denies any connection with Iran.[8] Prospective sanctions are likely to deter arms manufacturers from filling the many needs of the Iranian military.

The Iranian copy of the AT-3 is made by the Shahid Shah Abaday Industrial Group in Tehran. There are reports that it may be an early version of the missile that lacks semiautomatic guidance that allows the operator to simply sight the target, rather than use a joystick to guide the missile to the target by using the light from the missile to track it. These same reports indicate that the Iranian version seems to have a maximum armored penetration capability of 500 mm, which is not enough to penetrate the forward armor of the latest Western and Russian main battle tanks.

Russia has, however, refitted most of its systems to semiautomatic line-of-sight guidance and with tandem warheads capable of penetrating 800 mm. Iran may have or be acquiring such capabilities, which would significantly improve the lethality of its antiarmor forces. Recent reporting on Iranian arms transfers to Lebanon indicates that Iran does have AT-3s with advanced guidance systems and either an advanced Russian warhead or one designed by Raad engineers in Iran.[9]

IRANIAN ARTILLERY STRENGTH

Iran has some 3,000 to 3,200 operational medium and heavy artillery weapons and multiple rocket launchers, and some 5,000 mortars. Its towed artillery consists largely of effective Soviet designs. Its self-propelled artillery includes 60 2S1 122 mm weapons and some Iranian copies. It has some 180 aging M-109 155 mm weapons and again is seeking to produce its own weapons as part of the "Thunder" series. It has some 60 aging 170 mm, 165 mm, and 203 mm weapons. Iran also has large numbers of multiple rocket launchers, including some 700 107 mm weapons, 150 to 200 122 mm weapons, 20-odd 240 mm weapons, and some 333 mm weapons. It manufactures its own multiple rocket launchers, including the long-range Fajr series.

This total is very high by regional standards, and it reflects Iran's continuing effort to build up artillery strength that began during the Iran-Iraq War. Iran used artillery to support its infantry and IRGC in their attacks on Iraqi forces. Iran had to use artillery as a substitute for armor and airpower during much of the Iran-Iraq War, and it generally used relatively static massed fires. However, Iran's reliance on towed artillery and slow-moving multiple rocket launchers limits Iran's combined arms maneuver capabilities, and Iran has failed to develop effective night and beyond-visual-range targeting capability.

Some 2,085 of Iran's weapons are towed tube artillery weapons, versus 310 self-propelled tube weapons, and 700 to 900 vehicle-mounted or towed multiple rocket launchers. Iran's holdings of self-propelled weapons still appear to include a substantial number of U.S.-supplied systems, including 25 to 30 M-110 203 mm howitzers, 20 to 30 M-107 175 mm guns, and 130 to 150 M-109 155 mm howitzers. These U.S.-supplied weapons are worn, have not been modernized in more than 15 years, and lack modern fire control systems and artillery types of radar. Many lack sustainability, and a number may not be operational.

Iran understands that it has less than a quarter of the self-propelled artillery it needs to properly support its present force structure and that maneuverable artillery is critical to success in dealing with Iraqi and other maneuver forces. It is attempting to compensate for the resulting lack of modern artillery and artillery mobility by replacing its U.S. self-propelled weapons with other self-propelled systems. Iran has purchased 60 to 80 Soviet 2S1 122 mm self-propelled howitzers, and it has developed an Iranian-made design called the Raad (Thunder 1) and Raad (Thunder 2). The Thunder 1 is a 122 mm weapon similar to Russian designs. The Thunder 2 is a "rapid fire" 155 mm self-propelled weapon. Both systems are now in deployment.

Iran bought large numbers of mortars during the Iran-Iraq War for the same reasons it bought large numbers of towed tube artillery weapons. Iran has some 5,000 weapons. Included in these 5,000 weapons are a number of 107 mm and 120 mm heavy mortars and 800 to 900 81 mm and 82 mm mortars. Iran mounts at least several hundred of its heavy mortars on armored vehicles.

Iran's emphasis on massed, static area fire is also indicated by the fact it has 700 to 900 multiple rocket launchers, It is difficult to estimate Iran's inventory, but its holdings include roughly 10 M-1989 240 mm multiple rocket launchers, 500 to 700 Chinese Type 63 and Iranian Haseb and Fadjir-1 107 mm multiple rocket launchers, and more than 100 Soviet BM-21 and Soviet BM-11 122 mm launchers.

Iran has produced its own multiple rocket launchers. These include some 50 122 mm, 40 round Hadid rocket launcher systems. In addition, Iran is producing variants of Chinese and Russian 122 mm rockets called the Arash and Noor. Iranian state television announced the production of the DM-3b seeker for the Noor. The DM-3b is an active radar sensor that is used in the final stages of flight to acquire and home in on ship targets. A joint program between Iran's Aerospace Industries Organization and the China Aerospace Science and Industry Corporation developed the Noor.[10] The Falaq 1 and 2 series are examples of vehicle-mounted unguided rocket systems in the Iranian arsenal. The Falaq 1 fires a 240 mm rocket with 50 kilograms (kg) of explosives and can reach a target up to 10 km away. The Falaq 2 is slightly larger, carries 10 more kg of explosives, and flies almost a full kilometer further.[11]

Iran's land forces operate a number of Iranian-made long-range unguided rockets, including the Shahin 1 and 2, Oghab, and Nazeat. They also include some 10 large 240 mm artillery rockets with a range of up to 40 to 43 km called the Fadjr 3. The key longer-range systems seem to include: [12]

- The Shahin 1 (sometimes called the Fadjr 4) is a trailer-launched 333 mm caliber unguided artillery rocket. Two rockets are normally mounted on each trailer, and they have with a solid propelled rocket motor, a maximum range of 75 km, and a 175 kg conventional or chemical warhead. The Shahin evidently can be equipped with three types of warheads: a 180 kg high-explosive warhead, a warhead using high-explosive submunitions, and a warhead using chemical weapons. There is a truck-mounted version, called the Fajr 5, with a rack of four rockets. A larger Shanin 2, with a range of 20 km, is also deployed.

- The Fadjr-3 is a truck-mounted system with a 12 round launcher for 240 mm rockets. It has a maximum range of 43 km and a 45 kg payload in its warhead.

- The Fadjr 5 is truck-mounted 333 mm caliber unguided artillery rocket with a solid propelled rocket motor, a maximum range of 75 km, and a 175 kg conventional or chemical warhead. It carries four rockets, and they can evidently be equipped with three types of warheads: a high-explosive warhead, a warhead using high-explosive submunitions, and a warhead that uses chemical weapons.

- The Oghab is a 320 mm caliber unguided artillery rocket that is spin stabilized in flight, has a maximum range of 34 km, and a 70 kg high-explosive fragmentation warhead—although chemical warheads may be available. Though it may have a chemical warhead, it has an operational circular area probable (CEP) that has proved to be in excess of 500 meters at maximum range. Further, Iran has no way to target accurately the Oghab or any other long-range missile against mobile or point targets at long ranges, other than a limited ability to use remotely piloted vehicles (RPVs).

- The Nazeat is a transporter-erector-launcher (TEL)–launched system with conventional and possibly chemical and biological warheads. The full details of this system remain unclear, but it seems to be based on Chinese technology and uses a solid-fuel rocket, with a simple inertial guidance system. Nazeat units are equipped with communications vans, meteorological vans, and a global positioning system for surveying the launch site. Some reports indicate there are two variants of the Nazeat solid-fueled rocket system—a 355.6 mm caliber rocket with 105 km range and a 150 kg warhead, and a 450 mm caliber rocket with a reported range of 130 to 150 km and a 250 kg warhead. Both systems have maximum closing velocities of Mach 4 to 5, but both also appear to suffer from poor reliability and accuracy. Other reports indicate all Nazeats are 335.6 mm and there are four versions of progressively larger size, with ranges from 80 to 120 km. It is claimed to have a CEP within 5 percent of its range.

- The Zelzal 2 is a 610 mm long-range rocket, with a warhead with a 600 kg payload and a maximum range of up to 210 km. A single rocket is mounted on a launcher on a truck. It is unguided but is spin stabilized, and it is claimed to have a CEP within 5 percent of its range.

- The Fateh A-110 is a developmental system believed to be similar to the Chinese CSS-8, which is a surface-to-surface system derived from the Russian SA-2 surface-to-air missile.

Iran has only limited artillery fire control and battle management systems, counterbattery radar capability, and long-range target acquisition capability (although it does have some RPVs) to support its self-propelled weapons. Iran has actively sought more modern fire control and targeting systems since the mid-1980s. It has had some success in deploying and testing RPVs as targeting systems, and it has obtained some additional counterbattery radars, but it is unclear how many it has obtained or put in service.

Iran has transferred large numbers of Fadjr rockets to Hizballah in Lebanon.[13]

IRANIAN SURFACE-TO-SURFACE MISSILES

Iran continues to deploy surface-to-surface missiles, and it has its own systems in development. The number assigned to the army versus the IRGC is unclear, but the IRGC seems to hold and operate most long-range missiles rather than the army. Iran seems to have some 12 to 18 Scud B/C launchers and 250 to 350 missiles, and 30 land-based CSS-8 launchers with 175 missiles. Iran refers to the Scud B as the Shahab-1 and the Scud C as the Shahab-2.

Iran's Scud B Missiles

The Soviet-designed Scud B (17E) guided missile currently forms the core of Iran's ballistic missile forces:

- Iran acquired its Scuds in response to Iraq's invasion. It obtained a limited number from Libya and then obtained larger numbers from North Korea. It deployed these units with a special Khatam ol-Anbya force attached to the air element of the Pasdaran. Iran fired its first Scuds in March 1985. It fired as many as 14 Scuds in 1985, 8 in 1986, 18 in 1987, and 77 in 1988. Iran fired 77 Scuds during a 52-day period in 1988, during what came to be known as the "war of the cities." Sixty-one were fired at Baghdad, 9 at about

1 missile a day, and Iran was down to only 10 to 20 Scuds when the war of the cities ended.

- Iran's missile attacks were initially more effective than Iraq's attacks. This was largely a matter of geography. Many of Iraq's major cities were comparatively close to its border with Iran, but Tehran and most of Iran's major cities that had not already been targets in the war were outside the range of Iraqi Scud attacks. Iran's missiles, in contrast, could hit key Iraqi cities like Baghdad. This advantage ended when Iraq deployed extended-range Scuds.

- The Scud B is a relatively old Soviet design that first became operational in 1967, designated as the R-17E or R-300E. The Scud B has a range of 290–300 km with its normal conventional payload. The export version of the missile is about 11 meters long, is 85–90 centimeters in diameter, and weighs 6,300 kg. It has a nominal CEP of 1,000 meters. The Russian versions can be equipped with conventional high-explosive, fuel-air-explosive, runway penetrator, submunition, chemical, and nuclear warheads.

- The export version of the Scud B comes with a conventional high-explosive warhead weighing about 1,000 kg, of which 800 kg are the high-explosive payload and 200 are the warhead structure and fusing system. It has a single stage storable liquid rocket engine and is usually deployed on the MAZ-543 eight-wheel TEL. It has a strap-down inertial guidance, using three gyros to correct its ballistic trajectory, and it uses internal graphite jet vane steering. The warhead hits at a velocity above Mach 1.5.

- Most estimates indicate that Iran now has 6 to 12 Scud launchers and up to 200 Scud B (R-17E) missiles with a 230–310 km range.

- Some estimates give higher figures. They estimate that Iran bought 200 to 300 Scud Bs from North Korea between 1987 and 1992, and it may have continued to buy such missiles after that time. Israeli experts estimate that Iran had at least 250 to 300 Scud B missiles and at least 8 to 15 launchers on hand in 1997.

- U.S. experts also believe that Iran can now manufacture virtually all of the Scud B, with the possible exception of the most sophisticated components of its guidance system and rocket motors. This makes it difficult to estimate how many missiles Iran has in inventory and can acquire over time, as well as to estimate the precise performance characteristics of Iran's missiles, because it can alter the weight of the warhead, adjust the burn time, and improve the efficiency of the rocket motors.

Iran's Scud C Missiles

Iran also has longer-range North Korean Scuds—with ranges near 500 km. According to some reports, Iran has created shelters and tunnels in its coastal areas that it could use to store Scuds and other missiles in hardened sites to reduce their vulnerability to air attack. Iran's missile developments and features are as follows:

- The North Korean missile system is often referred to as a "Scud C." Typically, Iran formally denied the fact it had such systems long after the transfer of these missiles became a fact. Hassan Taherian, an Iranian foreign ministry official, stated in February 1995, "There is no missile cooperation between Iran and North Korea whatsoever. We deny this."

- In fact, a senior North Korean delegation traveled to Tehran to close the deal on November 29, 1990, and met with Mohsen Rezaei, the former commander of the IRGC. Iran either bought the missile then or placed its order shortly thereafter. North Korea then exported the missile through its Lyongaksan Import Corporation. Iran imported some of these North Korean missile assemblies using its B-747s, and it seems to have used ships to import others.

- Iran probably had more than 60 of the longer-range North Korean missiles by 1998, although other sources report 100, and one source reports 170.

- Iran may have 5 to 10 Scud C launchers, each with several missiles. This total seems likely to include 4 new North Korean TELs received in 1995.

- Iran seems to want enough missiles and launchers to make its missile force highly dispersible.

- Iran has begun to test its new North Korean missiles. There are reports that it has fired them from mobile launchers at a test site near Qom about 310 miles (500 km) to a target area south of Shahroud. There are also reports that units equipped with such missiles have been deployed as part of Iranian exercises like the Saeqer-3 (Thunderbolt 3) exercise in late October 1993.

- The missile is more advanced than the Scud B, although many aspects of its performance are unclear. North Korea seems to have completed development of the missile in 1987, after obtaining technical support from China. Though it is often called a "Scud C," it seems to differ substantially in detail from the original Soviet Scud B. It seems to be based more on the Chinese-made DF-61 than on a direct copy of the Soviet weapon.

- Experts estimate that the North Korean missiles have a range of about 310 miles (500 km), a warhead with a high-explosive payload of 700 kg, and relatively good accuracy and reliability. Though this payload is a bit limited for the effective delivery of chemical agents, Iran might modify the warhead to increase the payload at the expense of range and restrict the using of chemical munitions to the most lethal agents such as persistent nerve gas. It might also concentrate its development efforts on arming its Scud C forces with more lethal biological agents. In any case, such missiles are likely to have enough range-payload to give Iran the ability to strike all targets on the southern coast of the Gulf and all the populated areas in Iraq, although not the West. Iran could also reach targets in part of eastern Syria and the eastern third of Turkey, and it could cover targets in the border area of the former Soviet Union, western Afghanistan, and western Pakistan.

- Accuracy and reliability remain major uncertainties, as does operational CEP. Much would also depend on the precise level of technology Iran deployed in the warhead. Neither Russia nor China seems to have transferred the warhead technology for biological and chemical weapons to Iran or Iraq when they sold them the Scud B missile and CSS-8. However, North Korea may have sold Iran such technology as part of the Scud C sale. If it did so, such a technology transfer would save Iran years of development and testing in obtaining highly lethal biological and chemical warheads. In fact, Iran would probably be able to deploy far more effective biological and chemical warheads than Iraq had at the time of the Gulf War.

- Iran may be working with Syria in such development efforts, although Middle Eastern nations rarely cooperate in such sensitive areas. Iran served as a transshipment point for North Korean missile deliveries during 1992 and 1993. Some of this transshipment took place using the same Iranian B-747s that brought missile parts to Iran. Others moved by sea. For example, a North Korean vessel called the *Des Hung Ho*, bringing missile parts for Syria, docked at Bandar Abbas in May 1992. Iran then flew these parts to Syria. An Iranian ship coming from North Korea and a second North Korean ship followed, carrying missiles and machine tools for both Syria and Iran. At least 20 of the North Korean missiles have gone to Syria from Iran, and production equipment seems to have been transferred to Iran and to Syrian plants near Hama and Aleppo.

■ Iran can now assemble Scud B and Scud C missiles using foreign-made components. It may soon be able to make entire missile systems and warhead packages in Iran.

Iran's Shahab Missiles

Iran's new Shahab-3 (Shihab, Sehob) series is a much larger missile that seems to be based on the design of the North Korean No Dong 1 or A and No Dong B missile, which some analysts claim were developed with Iranian financial support. It is based on North Korean designs and technology but is being developed and produced in Iran. This development effort is controlled and operated by the IRGC.

The Shahab-3 is a single-stage liquid-fueled missile. It is road mobile, and it is believed to be 16 meters long and 1.32 meters in diameter and to have a launch weight of 16,250 kg. Iran has discussed payloads using submunitions, but it seems more likely to be designed to carry a chemical, nuclear, or biological weapon.[14]

Its range-payload, accuracy, and reliability are matters of speculation. Its nominal range is believed to be 1,300 km—long enough to hit virtually any target in the Gulf as well as Israel—and its payload to be 1,000–1,200 kg. It can carry a warhead with a 550–700 kg payload. An analysis by John Pike of GlobalSecurity.org points out, however, that missiles—like combat aircraft—can make trade-offs between range and payload. For example, the No Dong B has a range of 1,560 km with a 760 kg warhead and of 1,350 km with a 1,158 kg warhead.

The Shahab-3 may now be in deployment, but possibly only in "test-bed" units. Some reports have claimed that the Shahab-3 was operational as early as 1999. Reports surfaced that the development of the Shahab-3 was completed in June 2003, and that it underwent "final" tests on July 7, 2003. However, the Shahab-3 underwent a total of only nine tests from inception through late 2003, and only four of them could be considered successful in terms of basic system performance. The missile's design characteristics also continued to evolve during these tests. A report from the U.S. Central Intelligence Agency to Congress, dated November 10, 2003, indicated that the upgrading of the Shahab-3 was still under way, and some sources indicate that Iran is now seeking a range of 1,600 km.

Iran conducted further major Shahab-3 tests on August 11, 2004, deploying it with a new, smaller, and "bottle-neck" warhead. This kind of warhead has a slower reentry than a cone-shaped warhead and has advantages using warheads containing chemical and biological agents. Another test took place on September 19, 2004, and the missile was paraded on September 21 covered in banners saying "we will crush America under our feet" and "wipe Israel off the map."[15]

Nasser Maleki, the head of Iran's aerospace industry, stated on October 7 that "very certainly we are going to improve our Shahab-3 and all of our other missiles." Tehran also claimed in September that the Shahab-3 could now reach targets up to 2,000 km away, presumably allowing the missiles to be deployed a greater distance away from Israel's air force and Jericho-2 ballistic missiles.[16] The IRGC political bureau chief, Yadollah Javani, stated that the Shahab-3 could be used to attack Israel's Dimona nuclear reactor.[17]

Iran performed another test on October 20, 2004, and this time Iran's defense minister, Ali Shamkani, claimed that it was part of an exercise. Iran's defense minister also claimed that Iran was now capable of mass producing the Shahab-3 on November 9, 2004, and that Iran reserved the option of preemptive strikes in defense of its nuclear sites. Shamkani also claimed shortly afterward that the Shahab-3 now had a range of more than 2,000 km (1,250 miles).[18]

Since that time, the Mujahideen-e Khalq (MEK) has claimed that Iran is developing a version of the Shahab with a range of 2,400 km (1,500 miles). Mortezar Ramandi, an official in the Iranian delegation to the United Nations, has denied that Iran is developing a missile with a range of more than 1,250 miles (2,000 km); the MEK has an uncertain record of accuracy in making such claims, and they cannot be confirmed.[19]

Discussions of the Shahab-3's accuracy and reliability are largely speculative. If the system uses older guidance technology and warhead separation methods, its CEP could be anywhere from 1,000 to 4,000 meters. If it uses newer technology, such as some of the most advanced Chinese technology, it could have a CEP as low as 250 to 800 meters. In any case, such CEP data are engineering estimates, and missile accuracy and reliability cannot be measured using technical terms like CEP, which are based on simulations and models, not tests. Such tests assume that the missile can be perfectly targeted at launch and performs perfectly through its final guidance phase, and then somewhat arbitrarily define CEP as the accuracy of 50 percent of the systems launched. True performance can only be derived from observing reliability under operational conditions and from correlating the actual point of impact with a known aim point.

As is the case with virtually all unclassified estimates of missile performance, the estimates of accuracy and CEP available from public sources are matters of speculation, and no such source has credibility in describing performance in real-world, war-fighting terms. This is not a casual problem, because the actual weaponization of a warhead requires extraordinarily sophisticated systems to detonate the warhead at the desired height of burst and to reliably disseminate the munitions or agent. Even the most sophisticated conventional submunitions are little more than area weapons if the missile accuracy and target location has errors in excess of 250 to 500 meters, and a unitary conventional explosive warhead without terminal guidance is little more that a psychological or terror weapon almost regardless of its CEP.

The effective delivery of chemical agents by either spreading the agent or the use of submunitions generally requires accuracies under 1,000 meters to achieve lethality against, even large point targets. Systems with biological weapons are inherently area weapons, but a 1,000 kg nominal warhead can carry so little agent that accuracies under 1,000 meters again become desirable. Nuclear weapons require far less accuracy, particularly if a "dirty" ground burst can be targeted within a reliable fallout area. There are, however, limits. For example, a regular fission weapon of some 20 kilotons requires accuracies under 2,500 to 3,000 meters for some kinds of targets like sheltered airfields or large energy facilities.

The CIA report, dated November 10, 2003, also stated that Iran was developing a "Shahab-4" ballistic missile with a range of 2,000 km and possibly up to 3,000 km with a small warhead. Such a missile could reach targets in Europe and virtually any target in the Middle East.

Various experts have claimed that the Shahab-4 is based on the North Korean No Dong 2 or three-stage Taepodong-1 missile, or even some aspects of the Russian SS-4, but has a modern digital guidance package rather than the 2,000 to 3,000 meter CEP of early missiles like the SS-4. Russian firms are believed to have sold Iran special steels for missile development, test equipment, shielding for guidance packages, and other technology. Iran's Shahid Hemmet Industrial Group is reported to have contracts with the Russian Central Aerohydrodynamic Institute, Rosvoorouzhenie, the Bauman Institute, and Polyus. It is also possible that Iran has obtained some technology from Pakistan.

There have also been Israeli reports of an Iranian effort to create a Shahab-5, with a 4,900–5,000 km range. These reports remain uncertain, and Israeli media and official sources have repeatedly exaggerated the nature and speed of Iranian efforts.

The Iranian government stated as early as 1999 that it was developing such a large missile body or launch vehicle for satellite launch purposes, however, and repeatedly denied that it is upgrading the Shahab-3 for military purposes. Iran also continued to claim that the program that the West refers to as "Shahab-4" is one aimed at developing a booster rocket for launching satellites into space. In January 2004, Iran's defense minister claimed that Iran would launch a domestically built satellite within 18 months.[20]

As of December 2004, some U.S. intelligence experts were firmly convinced that Iran was aggressively seeking to develop a nuclear warhead for the Shahab series, They mentioned that Iran was actively working on the physical package for such a warhead design, and they cited U.S. secretary of state Colin Powell's warning on November 17, 2004, that Iran was working on such developments. Powell had stated that Iran was "actively working on (nuclear delivery) systems. . . . You don't have a weapon until you put it in something that can deliver a weapon."[21] U.S. officials stated that this information did not come from Iranian opposition sources like the MEK.

IRANIAN ARMY AIR DEFENSE SYSTEMS

Iranian land forces have a total of some 1,700 antiaircraft guns, including 14.5 mm ZPU-2/4s, 23 mm ZSU-23-4s and ZU-23s, 35 mm

M-1939s, 37 mm Type 55s, and 57 mm ZSU-57-2s. Iran also has 100 to 180 Bofors L/70 40 mm guns and moderate numbers of Skyguard 35 mm twin antiaircraft guns (many of which may not be operational). Its largest holdings consist of unguided ZU-23-2s (which it can manufacture) and M-1939s.

It is unclear how many of these systems are really operational as air defense weapons, and most would have to be used to provide very-short-range "curtain fire" defense of small point targets. They would not be lethal against a modern aircraft using an air-to-ground missile or laser-guided weapon. The only notable exception is the ZSU-23-4 radar-guided antiaircraft gun. Iran has 50 to 100 fully operational ZSU-23-4s. The weapon has a short range and is vulnerable to electronic countermeasures, but it is far more lethal than Iran's unguided guns.

Iran has large numbers of SA-7 (Strela 2M), and SA-14 (Strela) man-portable surface-to-air missiles, and some SA-16s and HN-5/HQ-5 man-portable surface-to-air missiles. It had some U.S.-made Stinger man-portable surface-to-air missiles that it bought from Afghan rebels, but these may no longer be operational or may have been used for reverse engineering purposes. Iran also has some RBS-70 low-level surface-to-air missiles. Iran seems to be producing some version of the SA-7, perhaps with Chinese assistance. It is not clear whether Iran can do this in any large number. Iran's land-based air defense forces are also acquiring growing numbers of Chinese FM-80s, a Chinese variant of the French-designed Crotale.

IRANIAN ARMY AVIATION

Iran pioneered the regional use of army aviation and attack helicopters during the time of the shah, but it built up its holdings of helicopters far more quickly than it expanded its training and maintenance capability. As a result, it had a hollow force at the time the shah fell. Its inability since that time to obtain adequate spare parts and help in modernizing the aircraft has long made Iranian operational helicopter holdings uncertain.

The Iranian Army seems to retain 50 AH-1J Sea Cobra attack helicopters and 20 CH-47C, 110 to 130 Bell-214A, 30 to 35 AB-214C, 35 to 40 AB-205A, 10 AB-206, and 25 Mi-8/Mi-27 transport and utility helicopters. There are also reports that it signed orders for 4 Mi-17s in

1999 and 30 Mi-8s in 2001. These Western-supplied transport and support helicopters have low operational readiness, and they have little sustained sortie capability.

Iran is also seeking to create a significant RPV force that borrows in many ways from Israeli technical developments and doctrine. It has produced some such RPVs, such as the Mohajer series—and several exercise reports refer to their use. It has sold some of these systems to Hizballah, but insufficient data are available to assess this aspect of Iranian capabilities.

IRANIAN ARMY COMMAND, CONTROL, COMMUNICATIONS, COMPUTERS, AND INTELLIGENCE

Iranian Army communications have improved, as have Iranian battle management and communications exercises. They are now capable of better coordination between branches, the density of communications equipment has improved, and the functional lines of communication and command now place more emphasis on maneuver, quick reaction, and combined arms. However, Iranian battle management and communications capabilities appear to remain relatively limited.

Iran's holdings still consist largely of aging VHF radio, with some HF and UHF capability. This equipment cannot handle high traffic densities, and secure communications are poor. Iran still relies heavily on analogue data handling and manually switched telephone systems. It is, however, acquiring a steadily growing number of Chinese and Western encryption systems and some digital voice, fax, and telex encryption capability.

OTHER ASPECTS OF IRANIAN ARMY CAPABILITY

Iran's Army has improved its organization, doctrine, training, and equipment for land force operations. Iran still, however, is a slow-moving force with limited armored maneuver capability and artillery forces better suited to static defense and the use of mass fires that the efficient use of rapidly switched and well-targeted fire. Sustainability is limited, as are field recovery and repair capability. The overall quality of labor is mediocre because of a lack of adequate realistic training and a heavy reliance on conscripts.

The army has some capability for power projection and armored maneuver warfare, but it does not train seriously for long-range maneuver and does little training for amphibious warfare or deployment by sea. Its logistics, maintenance, and sustainment system is largely defensive and designed to support Iranian forces in defending Iran from local bases. It does not practice difficult amphibious operations, particularly "across the beach" operations. It could, however, deploy into Kuwait and cross the border into Iraq. It can also move at least brigade-sized mechanize units across the Gulf by amphibious ship and ferry if it does not meet significant naval and air opposition to any such movement. It lacks the air strength and naval air and missile defense capabilities to be able to defend such an operation.

Notes

[1] International Institute for Strategic Studies, *The Military Balance, 1997–1998* and *2004–2005* (London: International Institute for Strategic Studies); *Jane's Sentinel Security Assessment: The Gulf States*, "Iran," various editions.

[2] There are reports that the lighter and smaller formations in the regular army include an Airmobile Forces group created since the Iran-Iraq War, and which includes the 29th Special Forces Division, which was formed in 1993–1994, and the 55th Paratroop Division. There are also reports that the regular army and IRGC commando forces are loosely integrated into a corps of up to 30,000 men with integrated helicopter lift and air assault capabilities. The airborne and special forces are trained at a facility in Shiraz. These reports are not correct. Note that detailed unit identifications for Iranian forces differ sharply from source to source. It is unclear that such identifications are accurate, and now-dated wartime titles and numbers are often published, sometimes confusing brigade numbers with division numbers.

[3] No reliable data exist on the size and number of Iran's smaller independent formations.

[4] See *Jane's Armor and Artillery, 2002–2003* (London: Jane's Information Group, 2003), 47–54.

[5] The estimates of Iran's AFV and APC strength are based on interviews with Israeli, British, and U.S. civilian experts, and the International Institute for Strategic Studies, *Military Balance*, "Iran," various editions; *Jane's Sentinel Security Assessment: The Gulf States*, "Iran," various editions.

[6] See *Jane's Armor and Artillery, 2002–2003*, 173.

[7] Christopher Foss, "Iran Reveals Up-Armoured Boraq Carrier," *Jane's Defence Weekly*, April 9, 2003, http://jdw.janes.com; also see *Jane's Armor and Artillery, 2002–2003*, 309–331.

[8] Lyubov Pronina, "U.S. Sanctions Russian Firm for Alleged Iran Sales," *Defense News*, September 22, 2003.

[9] Riad Kahwah and Barabara Opall-Rome, "Hizbollah: Iran's Battle Lab," *Defense News*, December 13, 2004.

[10] Doug Richardson, "Iran's Raad Cruise Missile Enters Production," *Jane's Missiles and Rockets*, March 1, 2004.

[11] *Jane's Defence Weekly*, January 15, 2003.

[12] *International Defense Review*, July 1996; Anthony H. Cordesman, *Iran's Weapons of Mass Destruction* (Washington, D.C: CSIS, 1997).

[13] Amir Taheir, "The Mullah's Playground," *Wall Street Journal*, December 7, 2004.

[14] This assessment draws upon a number of sources. Key sources include GlobalSecurity.org, "Shehab 3. Zelzal 3," http://www.globalsecurity.org/wmd/world/iran/shahab-3.htm; GlobalSecurity.org, "Shahab-4," http://www.globalsecurity.org/wmd/world/iran/shahab-4.htm; Missilethreat.com, a project of the Claremont Institute, http://www.missilethreat.com/missiles/shahab-3_iran.html; Missilethreat.com, "Shahab 4," Project of the Claremont Institute, http://www.missilethreat.com/missiles/shahab-4_iran.html; and Federation of American Scientists, "Shahab-3/Zezal-3," http://www.fas.org/nuke/guide/iran/missile/shahab-3.htm.

[15] Spacewar.com, "News," September 20, 2004; *Haaretz*, September 20, 2004.

[16] "Iran Boasts Shahab-3 Is in Mass Production," *Jane's Missiles and Rockets*, November 19, 2004.

[17] Jane's Islamic Affairs Analyst, "Iran threatens to Abandon the NPT," September 29, 2004.

[18] Douglas Jehl, "Iran Reportedly Hides Work on a Long-Range Missile, *New York Times*, December 2, 2004.

[19] Douglas Jehl, "Iran Is Said to Work on New Missile," *International Herald Tribune*, December 2, 2004; Jehl, "Iran Reportedly Hides Work on a Long-Range Missile."

[20] "Iran Enhances Existing Weaponry by Optimising Shahab-3 Ballistic Missile," *Jane's Missiles and Rockets*, January 20, 2004.

[21] Bill Gertz, "US Told of Iranian Effort to Create Nuclear Warhead," *Washington Times*, December 2, 2004.

CHAPTER THREE

THE ISLAMIC REVOLUTIONARY GUARDS CORPS (THE PASDARAN)

The Islamic Revolutionary Guards Corps (IRGC), or the Pasdaran, adds some 120,000 additional men to Iran's armed forces. Roughly 100,000 are ground forces, including many conscripts. There are a large naval branch and a small air branch. Estimates of the IRGC's equipment strength are highly uncertain. The International Institute for Strategic Studies estimates that it has some 470 tanks, 620 armored personnel carriers, 360 artillery weapons, 40 multiple rocket launchers, and 150 air defense guns, but these estimates are now several years old.

The naval branch has some 20,000 men. According to the International Institute for Strategic Studies, this total includes Iran's marine of some 5,000 men, and a combat strength of one brigade. Other sources show this force subordinated to the Iranian Navy. It has at least 40 light patrol boats, 10 Houdong guided missile patrol boats armed with C-802 antiship missiles, and a battery of HY-2 Seersucker land-based antiship missiles. It has bases in the Gulf, many near key shipping channels and some near the Strait of Hormuz. These include facilities at Al-Farsiyah, Halul (an oil platform), Sirri, Abu Musa, Bandaer-e Abbas, Khorramshahr, and Larak. It also controls Iran's coastal defense forces, including naval guns and an HY-3 Seersucker land-based antiship missile unit deployed at five to seven sites along the Gulf coast.

These forces can carry out extensive raids against Gulf shipping, can carry out regular amphibious exercises with the land branch of the IRGC against objectives like islands in the Gulf, and could conduct raids against Saudi Arabia or other countries on the Southern Gulf coast. They give Iran a major capability for asymmetric warfare. The IRGC also seems to work closely with Iranian intelligence and seems to be represented unofficially in some embassies, in Iranian businesses and purchasing offices, and on other foreign fronts.

IRGC elements do seem to run training camps inside Iran for outside "volunteers." Some 400 IRGC troops seem to be deployed in Lebanon and actively involved in training and arming Hizballah, other anti-Israeli groups, and other elements.[1] The IRGC has been responsible for major arms shipments to Hizballah, including large numbers of AT-3 antitank guided missiles, long-range rockets, and some Iranian-made Mohajer unmanned aerial vehicles.[2] Some reports indicate Iran has sent thousands of 122 millimeter rockets and Fajr 4 and Fajr 5 long-range rockets, including the ARASH with a range of 21 to 29 kilometers. These reports give the Fajr 5 a range of 75 kilometers, with a payload of 200 kilograms. Iran seems to have sent arms to various Palestinian movements, including some shiploads of arms to the Palestinian Authority.[3]

As has been touched upon above, the air branch is believed to operate Iran's three Shahab-3 intermediate-range ballistic missile units, and it may have had custody of its chemical weapons and any biological weapons. Though the actual operational status of the Shahab-3 remains uncertain, Iran's supreme leader, the Ayatollah Ali Khamenei, announced in 2003 that Shahab-3 missiles had been delivered to the IRGC. In addition, six Shahab-3s were displayed in Tehran during a military parade in September 2003.[4]

Sources differ sharply on the organization of the IRGC, and its combat formations seem to be much smaller than its name implies, and to differ sharply from unit to unit. The International Institute for Strategic Studies reports a strength of 2 armored, 5 mechanized, 10 infantry, and 1 Special Forces division, plus 15 to 20 independent brigades, including some armed and paratroop units. In practice, its manning would support 3 to 5 real divisions, and many of its divisions have an active strength equivalent to large brigades.

The IRGC has a complex structure that is both political and military. It has separate organizational elements for its land, naval, and air units, which include both military and paramilitary units. The Basij and the tribal units of the Pasdaran are subordinated to its land unit command, although the commander of the Basij often seems to report directly to the commander-in-chief and minister of the Pasdaran and through him to the leader of the Islamic Revolution. The

IRGC has close ties to the foreign operations branch of the Iranian Ministry of Intelligence and Security, particularly through the IRGC's Qods force. The Ministry of Intelligence and Security was established in 1983, and it has an extensive network of offices in Iranian embassies. It is often difficult to separate the activities of the IRGC, VEVAK, and Foreign Ministry, and many seem to be integrated operations managed by a ministerial committee called the Special Operations Council that includes the leader of the Islamic Revolution, the president, the minister of intelligence and security, and other members of the Supreme Council for National Defense.[5]

The IRGC's growing involvement in Iran's military industries, and its lead role in Iran's efforts to acquire surface-to-surface missiles and weapons of mass destruction, give it growing experience with advanced military technology. As a result, the IRGC is believed to be the branch of Iran's forces that plays the largest role in Iran's military industries.[6] It also operates all of Iran's Scuds, controls most its chemical and biological weapons, and provides the military leadership for missile production and the production of all weapons of mass destruction.

The IRGC plays a major role in internal security. Nevertheless, it seems best to treat the IRGC primarily as a military land force that parallels the Iranian regular army, and that would operate with it in most contingencies. As discussed above, the IRGC has been placed under an integrated command with Iran's regular armed forces at the General Staff level. It retains an independent command chain below this level, however, and generally continues to exercise as an independent force. It rarely exercises with the regular Iranian army—and then usually in large, set piece exercises that do not require close cooperation.[7]

It is difficult to estimate the proficiency of IRGC units. It seems likely, however, that they vary sharply by unit and that only a portion of the IRGC land forces are intended to participate in joint operations with the regular army in regular combat. These forces seem to have improved steadily in their training, organization, and discipline since the early 1990s, and they have also expanded their joint training with the regular army, navy, and air force.

The IRGC would probably be capable of providing an extensive defense capability in the event of any invasion of Iran. It is also light enough so that its units could rapidly deploy as "volunteers" to Iraq or any Southern Gulf country, where they could obtain local support and access to a seaport or airport. It seems likely that they could move into a country like Iraq in significant force—at least several brigade equivalents and possibly at the division level—if they were invited to do so by some friendly faction. They could also infiltrate in significant numbers. It seems unlikely that the IRGC could deploy and sustain more than a force of several brigades if it were invited into a secure port by some Southern Gulf faction and were not opposed by air and sea. It could certainly mount a significant attack on any island or off-shore facility in the Gulf and covertly or overtly introduce large numbers of free-floating or bottom mines into any shipping channel.

THE QUDS (QODS) FORCE

The IRGC has a large intelligence operations and unconventional warfare component. Roughly 5,000 of the men in the IRGC are assigned to the unconventional warfare mission. The IRGC has the equivalent of one Special Forces "division," plus additional smaller formations, and these forces are given special priority for training and equipment. In addition, the IRGC has a special Quds force, which plays a major role in giving Iran the ability to conduct unconventional warfare overseas using various foreign movements as proxies. This force is under the command of General Ahmad Vahidi (Wahidi), who used to head the information department in the IRGC General Command and had the mission of exporting the revolution.[8]

The budget for the Quds force is classified, is directly controlled by Khamenei, and is not reflected in the Iranian general budget. The Quds operates primarily outside Iran's borders, although it has bases inside and outside of Iran. The Quds troops are divided into specific groups or "corps" for each country or area in which they operate. There are Directorates for Iraq; Lebanon, Palestine, and Jordan; Afghanistan, Pakistan, and India; Turkey and the Arabian Peninsula; and the Asiatic republics of the former Soviet Union, Western Nations (Europe and North America), and North Africa (Egypt, Tunisia, Algeria, Sudan, and Morocco).

The Quds has offices or "sections" in many Iranian embassies, which are closed to most embassy staff. It is not clear whether these are integrated with Iranian intelligence operations or that the ambassador in such embassies has control—or detailed knowledge—of operations by the Quds staff. However, there are indications that most operations are coordinated between the IRGC and offices within the Iranian Foreign Ministry and Ministry of Intelligence and Security. There are separate operational organizations in Lebanon, Turkey, Pakistan, and several North African countries. There also indications that such elements may have participated in the bombings of the Israeli Embassy in Argentina in 1992, and the Jewish Community Center in Buenos Aires in 1994—although Iran has strongly denied this.[9]

The Quds force seems to control many of Iran's training camps for unconventional warfare, extremists, and terrorists in Iran and countries like the Sudan and Lebanon. It has at least four major training facilities in Iran. The Quds has a main training center at Imam Ali University that is based in the Sa'dabad Palace in Northern Tehran. Troops are trained to carry out military and terrorist operations, and they are indoctrinated in ideology. There are other training camps in the Qom, Tabriz, and Mashhad governates, and in Lebanon and the Sudan. These include the Al Nasr camp for training Iraqi Shi'ites and Iraqi and Turkish Kurds in northwest Iran, and a camp near Mashhad for training Afghan and Tajik revolutionaries. The Quds seems to help operate the Manzariyah training center near Qom, which recruits from foreign students in the religious seminary and which seems to have trained some Bahraini extremists. Some foreigners are reported to have received training in demolition and sabotage at an IRGC facility near Esfahan, in airport infiltration at a facility near Mashad and Shiraz, and in underwater warfare at an IRGC facility at Bandar Abbas.[10]

THE BASIJ AND OTHER PARAMILITARY FORCES

The rest of Iran's paramilitary and internal security forces seem to have relatively little war-fighting capability. The Basij (Mobilization of the Oppressed) is a popular reserve force of about 90,000 men with an active and reserve strength of up to 300,000 and a mobilization capacity of nearly 1,000,000 men. It is controlled by the IRGC, and it consists largely of youths, men who have completed military service, and the elderly. It has up to 740 regional battalions with about 300 to

350 men each, which are composed of three companies or four platoons plus support. These include the former tribal levies and are largely regional in character. Many have little or no real military training and full-time active manning. However, Iran has used the Basij to provide local security ever since the popular riots of 1994. It called up more than 100,000 men in 19 regions in September 1994, and it began far more extensive training for riot control and internal security missions. It also introduced a formal rank structure and a more conventional system of command and discipline, and it created specialized Ashura battalions for internal security missions. Some reports indicate that 36 of these battalions were established in 1994. The primary missions of the Basij now seem to be internal security, monitoring the activities of Iranian citizens, acting as replacements for the military services, and serving as a static militia force tied to local defense missions.

Iran also has 45,000 to 60,000 men in the Ministry of the Interior serving as police and border guards, with light utility vehicles, light patrol aircraft (Cessna 185/310 and AB-205 and AB-206s), 90 coastal patrol craft, and 40 harbor patrol craft.

Notes

[1] Riad Kahwah and Barabara Opall-Rome, "Hizbollah: Iran's Battle Lab," *Defense News*, December 13, 2004.

[2] Amir Taheir, "The Mullah's Playground," *Wall Street Journal*, December 7, 2004.

[3] The estimates of such holdings of rockets are now in the thousands, but the numbers are very uncertain. Dollar estimates of what are significant arms shipments are little more than analytic rubbish, based on cost methods that border on the absurd, but significant shipments are known to have taken place.

[4] "Iran Enhances Existing Weaponry by Optimising Shahab-3 Ballistic Missile," *Jane's Missiles and Rockets*, January 20, 2004.

[5] See *Time*, March 21, 1994, and November 11, 1996. Also see *Washington Post*, November 21, 1993, August 22, 1994, October 28, 1994, November 27, 1994, April 11, 1997, and April 14, 1997; *Los Angeles Times*, November 3, 1994; Deutsche Presse-Agentur, April 17, 1997; Reuters, April 16, 1997, and April 17, 1997; *The European*, April 17, 1997; *The Guardian*, October 30, 1993, August 24, 1996, and April 16, 1997; *New York Times*, April 11, 1997; Associated Press, April 14, 1997; *Jane's Defence Weekly*, June 5, 1996; Agence France Press, April 15, 1997;

BBC, April 14, 1997; Deustcher Depeschen via ADN, April 12, 1997; and *Washington Times*, April 11, 1997.

[6] For typical reporting by officers of the IRGC on this issue, see the comments of its acting commander in chief, Brigadier General Seyyed Rahim Safavi, speaking to reporters during IRGC week, December 20–26, 1995. FBIS-NES-95-250, December 25, 1995, IRNA 1406 GMT.

[7] Interviews and *Washington Times*, May 12, 1997, and October 11, 1997; *Jane's Defence Weekly*, June 25, 1997, and October 1, 1997; Reuters, July 3, 1997, July 9, 1997, September 28, 1997, and October 6, 1997.

[8] The reader should be aware that much of the information relating to the Quds is highly uncertain and is drawn from Israeli sources. Also, however, see the article from the Jordanian publication *Al-Hadath* in FBIS-NES-96-108, May 27, 1996; and in *Al-Sharq Al-Awsat*, FBIS-NES-96-110, June 5, 1996; A. J. Venter, "Iran Still Exporting Terrorism," *Jane's Intelligence Review*, November 1997.

[9] *New York Times*, May 17, 1998; *Washington Times*, May 17, 1998; *Washington Post*, May 21, 1998.

[10] Venter, "Iran Still Exporting Terrorism."

CHAPTER FOUR

THE IRANIAN NAVY

The Iranian Navy has some 18,000 men. According to the International Institute for Strategic Studies, this total includes a two-brigade marine force of some 2,600 men and a naval aviation force of 2,000 men. It has bases at Bandar-e Abbas, Bushehr, Kharg Island, Bander-e Anzelli, Chah Bahar, Bander-e Mahshahar, and Bander-e Khomeini. This gives it bases opposing most of the Saudi Arabian coast.

It has 3 submarines, 3 frigates, 2 corvettes, 10 missile patrol craft, 7 mine warfare ships, 44 coastal and inshore patrol craft, and 9 to 10 amphibious ships. Its naval aviation branch is one of the few air elements in any Gulf Navy, and it has 5 maritime patrol aircraft and 19 armed helicopters. When combined with the naval branch of the Islamic Revolutionary Guards Corps (IRGC), this is a total maritime strength of 38,000 men with significant capabilities for both regular naval and asymmetric naval warfare. Table 4.1 provides the details of the development of the force structure in the Iranian navy since the Iran-Iraq War in 1989, levels of labor power, and numbers and types of major weapons.

Iran has given the modernization of its naval forces high priority, although its major surface ships are all old vessels with limited refits and aging weapons and fire control systems. Since the end of the Iran-Iraq War, Iran has obtained new antiship missiles and missile patrol craft from China, midget submarines from North Korea, submarines from Russia, and modern mines. Iran has expanded the capabilities of the naval branch of the IRGC, acquired additional mine warfare capability, and upgraded some of its older surface ships. Iran's exercises

Table 4.1
Iran's Navy: Force Structure Trends, 1989–2005

Aspect of Force Structure	1989–1990	1999–2000	2004–2005
Labor power	14,500	20,600	18,000
Navy	?	18,000	15,400
Marines	?	2,600	2,600
Destroyers	3	0	0
Damavand (UK Battle)	1	0	0
Badr	2	0	0
Submarines	0	5	3
SSI0	2	0	
SSK: Kilo (RF Type 877)	0	3	3
Frigates	3	3	3
FFG: Alvand (UK Vosper Mk 5)	3	3	3
Corvettes	2	2	2
Bayandor	2	2	2
Missile craft	10	20	10
Houdong	0	10	0
Kaman	10	10	10
Patrol coastal	0	3	3
Parvin PCC	0	3	3
Patrol inshore	6+	42	41
Parvin PCI	3	0	0
Zafar PCI<	0	3	3
Bogomol PFI	0	1	0
China Cat PCI<	0	?	3
CH Chaho PFI	3	0	0
PFI	0	35	35
Hovercraft	15	9	14
Small craft	?	60+	100+
Mine layers: Hejaz LST	?	2	2
Mine countermeasures	3	5	5
Shahrokh	2	1	1
Harischi MSI	1	0	0
292 MSC	0	2	2
Riazi	0	2	2

(continued next page)

(Table 4.1, continued)

Aspect of Force Structure	1989–1990	1999–2000	2004–2005
Amphibious	7	9	10
Hengram LST	4	4	4
Iran Hormuz	3	3	3
Fouque LSL	0	2	3
Plus craft	4	9	9
LCT	4	3	3
ACV	0	6	6
Support	8	25	25
Bandar Abbas AOR	2	2	2
Repair	1	0	0
Accommodation Vessels	2	0	0
Water Tankers	2	0	0
Kharg AO	1	1	1
AWT	0	0	2
Delvar Support	0	7	5
Hendijan Support	0	9	12
AT	0	1	1
Training Craft	0	1	2
MR aircraft	0	8	10
P-3F	0	3	5
Do-228	0	5	5
Transportation aircraft	8	8	8
Commander	4	4	4
F-27	4	4	4
Antisubmarine warfare helicopters	9	9	20
SH-3D	3	3	10
AB-212	6	6	10
MCM helicopters	2	2	3
RH-53D	2	2	3
Transportation helicopters	1+	1+	10
Falcon 20	1	1	3
AB 205a	?	?	5
AB-206	?	?	2

Source: Adapted by Anthony H. Cordesman from International Institute for Strategic Studies, *The Military Balance* (London: International Institute for Strategic Studies, various years).

Note: A "?" means that the International Institute for Strategic Studies does not report the exact number; a "+" means that number or greater; a "<" means less than 100 tons.

have included a growing number of joint and combined arms exercises with the land forces and air force.

Iran has also improved its ports and strengthened its air defenses, while obtaining some logistic and technical support from nations like India and Pakistan. In August 2000, Iran announced that it had launched its first domestically produced light submarine, which is called the Al-Sabiha 15. It can be used for reconnaissance and laying mines.[1]

IRANIAN ANTISHIP MISSILES AND MISSILE CRAFT

Iran's depends heavily on its ability to use antiship missiles to make up for its lack of airpower and modern major surface vessels. Iran's Western-supplied missiles are now all beyond their shelf life, and their operational status is uncertain. Iranian forces are now operating four systems that Iran has obtained from China:

- *The Seersucker* is a long-range, mobile antiship missile, which is designated the HY-2 or Sea Eagle-2 by China. It is a large missile with a 0.76 meter diameter and a weight of 3,000 kilograms (kg). It has a range of 80 to 90 kilometers (km) and a 450 kg warhead. There are two variants. One uses radar active homing at ranges from the target of 8 km (4.5 nautical miles). The other uses passive infrared homing and a radar altimeter to keep it at a constant height over the water.

- *The CS-801* antiship missile, also called the Yinji (Hawk) missile, is a solid-fueled missile. It can be launched from land and ships. It has a range of approximately 74 km in the surface-to-surface mode, and it uses J-Band active radar guidance. It has a 512 kg warhead and cruises at an altitude of 20 to 30 meters.

- *The CS-802* is an upgraded CS-801. It uses a turbojet propulsion system with a rocket booster instead of the solid-fueled booster in the CS-801. It has a range of 70 to 75 miles, has a warhead of up to 363 pounds, and can be targeted by a radar deployed on a smaller ship or aircraft operating over the radar horizon of the launching vessel.[2]

- *The CS-801K* is a Chinese-supplied, air-launched antiship missile and variant of the CS-801. It too is a sea-skimming, high-subsonic cruise missile, and it has a range in excess of 20 nautical miles. It has been test fired by Iran's F-4Es, but Iran may be able to use other launch aircraft. This air delivery capability gives Iran what some analysts have called a "360 degree" attack capability, because aircraft can rapidly maneuver to far less predictable launch points than Iranian combat ships.[3]

Iran has sought to buy advanced antiship missiles from Russia, North Korea, and China and to buy antiship missile production facilities, and possibly even Chinese-made missile armed frigates. Some sources have claimed that Iran has bought eight Soviet-made SS-N-22 "Sunburn" or "Sunburst" antiship missile launch units from Ukraine and has deployed them near the Strait of Hormuz. However, U.S. experts have seen no evidence of such a purchase and doubt that Iran has any operational holdings of such systems. The "SS-N-22" is a title that actually applies to two different modern long-range supersonic sea-skimming systems—the P-270 Moskit (also called the Kh-15 or 3M80) and the P80 or P-100 Zubi/Onika.

Iran's main launch platforms for antiship missiles include three British-supplied Vosper Mark 5 Sa'am-class frigates—called the *Alvand*, *Alborz*, and *Sabalan*. These ships date back to the time of the shah, and each is a 1,100-ton frigate with a crew of 125 to 146 and maximum speeds of 39 knots. Each was originally armed with one five-missile Sea Killer Mark II surface-to-surface missile launcher and one Mark 8 4.5 inch gun mount. They have since had their Sea Killers replaced with C-802 antiship missiles and new fire control radars. The Sea Killer has a relatively effective beam-riding missile with radio command or optical guidance, and a maximum range of 25 km.

All three ships are active, but the *Sabalan* took serious damage from the U.S. Navy during the tanker war of 1987–1988, and the ships have not had a total refit since the early 1990s. The antisubmarine warfare (ASW) capabilities of these ships seem to be limited or non-functioning. Iran has two U.S. PF-103 (Bayandor-class) corvettes called the *Bayandor* and the *Naghdi*. These ships are 900-ton vessels, with crews of 140, two 76 millimeter (mm) guns, and a maximum speed of 18 knots. They were laid down in 1962 and delivered in 1964. The *Bayandor* and the *Naghdi* are probably the most active large surface ships in the Iranian navy. However, neither is equipped with antiship and antiair missiles, sophisticated weapons systems, sonars, or advanced electronic warfare equipment and sensors.[4] Iran is slowly building a 1,500-ton corvette, but its status is uncertain, as are its equipment and armament.

The rest of Iran's major surface vessels consist of missile patrol boats. These include 10 68-ton Chinese-built Thnodor (Hudong)–class fast attack craft or missile patrol boats. The Hudong class fast attack craft are equipped with I-band search and navigation radar but do not have a major antiair missile system. Iran ordered these ships for the naval branch of the IRGC in 1992, and all 10 were delivered to Iran by March 1996. The vessels have a crew of 28. They carry four antiship missiles and are armed with CS-801 and CS-802 missiles.

Iran now has at least 100 CS-801s and CS-802s. Iran's missile patrol boats also include 10 275-ton French-made Combattante II (Kaman-class) fast attack boats, out of an original total of 12. These boats are armed with antiship missiles, 1 76 mm gun, and have maximum speeds of 37.5 knots. They were originally armed with 4 US Harpoon missiles, but their Harpoons may no longer be operational. At least 5 had been successfully converted with launchers that can carry 2 to 4 CS-801/CS-802s.

Iran has a number of large patrol craft and fast attack craft. The operational ships of this type include three North Korean-supplied 82-ton Zafar-class (Chaho-class) fast attack craft with I-band search radar and armed with 23 mm guns and a BM-21 multiple rocket launcher; two Kavian-class (U.S. Cape-class) 148-ton patrol craft armed with 40 mm and 23 mm guns; and three Improved PGM-71 Parvin-class 98-ton patrol craft supplied in the late 1960s and armed with 40 mm and 20 mm guns.

There are more than 35 other small patrol boats plus large numbers of small boats operated by the IRGC. Most of these craft are operational and can be effective in patrol missions. However, they lack sophisticated weapons systems or air defenses, other than machine guns and SA-7s and SA-14s. Iran has 5 to 6 BH-7 and 7 to 8 SRN-6 Hovercraft, which are believed to be operated by the IRGC. About half of these Hovercraft may be operational. They are capable of speeds of up to 60 to 70 knots. They are lightly armed and vulnerable, but their high speed makes them useful for many reconnaissance and unconventional warfare missions, and they can rapidly land troops on suitable beaches.

IRANIAN MINE WARFARE CAPABILITIES

Mine warfare, amphibious warfare, antiship missiles, and unconventional warfare give Iran other ways of compensating for the weakness of its conventional air and naval forces. Iran's mine warfare vessels include two to three operational Shahrock-class MSC-292/268 coastal minesweepers (one used for training in the Caspian Sea). Two of these three ships, the *Shahrock* and *Karkas*, are known to be operational. They are 378-ton sweepers that can be used to lay mines as well as sweep, but their radar and sonar date back to the late 1950s and are obsolete in sweeping and countermeasure activity against modern mines.

Iran has one to two operational Cape-class (Riazzi-class) 239-ton inshore minesweepers, and it seems to have converted two of its Iran Ajar-class landing ships, tank (LSTs), for mine warfare purposes. Many of its small boats and craft can also lay mines. Both the Iranian Navy and the naval branch of the IRGC are expanding their capability for mine warfare. Though Iran has only a limited number of specialized mine vessels, it can also use small craft, LSTs, Boghammers, helicopters, and submarines to lay mines. As a result, it is impossible to determine how many ships Iran would employ to plant or lay mines in a given contingency, and some of its mines might be air dropped or laid by commercial vessels, including dhows.

Iran has a range of Soviet-, Western-, and Iranian-made moored and drifting contact mines, and U.S. experts estimate that Iran has at least 2,000 mines. Iran has significant stocks of antiship mines, and it has bought Chinese-made and North Korean–made versions of the Soviet mines. It has claimed to be making its own nonmagnetic, acoustic, free-floating, and remote-controlled mines, and it has had Chinese assistance in developing the production facilities for such mines. It may have acquired significant stocks of nonmagnetic mines, influence mines, and mines with sophisticated timing devices from other countries. [5]

There also are reports that Iran has negotiated with China to buy the EM-52 or MN-52 rocket-propelled mine. The EM-52 is a mine that rests on the bottom until it senses a ship passing over it, and it then uses a rocket to hit the target. The maximum depth of the Strait of Hormuz is 80 meters (264 feet), although currents are strong enough to displace all but firmly moored mines.[6] In combination with modern submarine-laid mines and antiship missile systems like the CS-801/802 and SS-N-22, the EM-52 would give Iran considerable capability to harass Gulf shipping and even the potential capability to close the Gulf until U.S. naval power and airpower could clear the mines and destroy the missile launchers and submarines.

Even obsolete moored mines have proven difficult to detect and sweep when intelligence does not detect the original laying and size of the minefield, and free-floating mines can be used to present a constant hazard to shipping. Bottom-influence mines can use acoustic, magnetic, or pressure sensors to detect ships passing overhead. They can use multiple types of sensors and actuators to make it hard to deceive the mines and force them to release, can be set to release only after a given number of ships pass, and some can be set to attack only ships of a given size or noise profile. Such mines are extremely difficult to detect and sweep, particularly when they are spaced at wide intervals in shipping lanes.

IRANIAN AMPHIBIOUS ASSETS

Iran has significant amphibious assets by Gulf standards, and the regular Iranian Navy and naval branch of the IRGC have independent marine forces. These assets, which are large enough to move a battalion-sized force relatively rapidly, include three Hengam-class (Larak-class) LST amphibious support ships (displacement of 2,940 tons loaded) that can carry up to six tanks, 600 tons of cargo, and 227 troops; three Iran Hormuz-class (South Korean) LSTs (2,014 tons loaded) that can carry up to nine tanks and berth 140 troops; and three Hormuz-21 class 1,80-ton LSTs and three Fouque class 176-ton LSLs.

Iran's amphibious ships give it the theoretical capability to deploy about 1,000 troops and about 30 to 40 tanks in an amphibious assault—but Iran has never demonstrated that it has an effective over-the-shore capability. Iran might use commercial ferries and roll-on/roll-off ships if it felt they could survive. Iran has also built up its capability to hide or shelter small ships in facilities on its islands and coastline along the Gulf, and its ability to provide them with defensive cover from antiair and antiship missiles. However, all of Iran's training to date has focused on amphibious raiding and not on operations using heavy weapons or larger operations. Iran lacks the air and surface power to move its amphibious forces across the Gulf in the face of significant air and sea defenses, or to support a landing in a defended area.

Iran has support ships, but these are generally insufficient to sustain "blue water" operations and support an amphibious task force. It has 1 Kharg-class 33,014-ton replenishment ship; 2 Bandar Abbas-class 4,673-ton fleet supply ships and oilers; 1 14,410-ton repair ship; 2 12,000-ton water tankers; 7 1,300-ton Delva-class support ships; 5 to 6 Hendijan-class support vessels; 2 floating drydocks; and 20 tugs, tenders, and utility craft to help support a large naval or amphibious operation.

IRANIAN NAVAL AIR

The Iranian Navy's air capability consists of 2 to 3 operational P-3F Orion maritime patrol aircraft out of an original inventory of 5. According to reports from the Gulf, none of the surviving P-3Fs have fully operational radars and their crews often use binoculars. It also has up to 12 Sikorsky SH-3D ASW helicopters, 2 RH-53D mine-laying helicopters, and 7 Agusta-Bell AB-212 helicopters. It uses air force AH-1J attack helicopters, equipped with French AS-12 missiles, in naval missions, and it has adapted Hercules C-130 and Fokker Friendship aircraft for mine-laying and patrol missions. The most significant recent development in Iran's capabilities to use airpower to attack naval targets has been the acquisition of the CS-801K for its regular air force.

IRAN'S SUBMARINE FORCES

Iran has attempted to offset the weakness of its major surface forces by obtaining three Type 877 EKM Kilo-class submarines. The Kilo is a relatively modern and quiet submarine that first became operational in 1980. The Iranian Kilos are Type 877 EKM export versions that are about 10 meters longer than the original Kilos and are equipped with advanced command-and-control systems. Each Type 877 EKM has a teardrop hull coated with anechoic tiles to reduce noise. It displaces approximately 3,076 tons when submerged and 2,325 tons when surfaced. It is 72.6 meters long, is 9.9 meters in beam, has a draught of 6.6 meters, and is powered by three 1,895 HP generator sets, one 5,900 SHP electric motor, and one six-bladed propeller. It has a complement of 52 men and an endurance of 45 days. Its maximum submerged speed is 17 knots, and its maximum surface speed is 10 knots.

Each Kilo has 6 530 mm torpedo tubes, including 2 wired-guided torpedo tubes. Only 1 torpedo can be wire guided at a time. The Kilo can carry a mix of 18 homing and wire-guided torpedoes or 24 mines. Russian torpedoes are available with ranges of 15 to 19 km, speeds of 29 to 40 knots, and warheads with weights of 100, 205, and 305 kg. Their guidance systems include active sonar homing, passive homing, wire guidance, and active homing. Some reports indicate that Iran bought more than 1,000 modern Soviet mines with the Kilos, and that the mines were equipped with modern magnetic, acoustic, and pressure sensors. The Kilo has a remote antiaircraft launcher with 1 preloaded missile in the sail, and Soviet versions have 6 SA-N-5 (Igla/SA-16) surface-to-air missiles stored inside. However, Russia only supplied Iran with the SA-14 (Strela). It can be modernized to carry Chinese YJ-1 or Russian Novator Alfa surface-to-surface missles.[7]

The Kilo has a maximum surface speed of 10 knots, a maximum submerged speed of about 17 knots, a minimum submerged operating depth of about 30 meters, an operational diving depth of 240 meters, and a maximum diving depth of 300 meters. The submarine also has a surface cruise range of 3,000 to 6,000 nautical miles and a submerged cruise range of 400 nautical miles—depending on speed and combat conditions.[8]

Iran's ability to use its submarines to deliver mines and fire long-range wake-homing torpedoes give it a potential capability to strike in ways that make it difficult to detect or attack the submarine. Mines can be laid covertly in critical areas before a conflict, and mines can be set to activate and deactivate at predetermined intervals in ways that make mining difficult to detect and sweep. Long-range homing torpedoes can be used against tanker-sized targets at ranges in excess of 10 km, and to attack slow-moving combat ships that are not on alert and/or that lack sonar and countermeasures.

At the same time, many countries in the developing world have found submarines to be difficult to operate. For example, Russia delivered the first two Kilos with two 120-cell batteries designed for rapid power surges, rather than power over long periods. They proved to last only one to two years in warm waters versus five to seven years for similar batteries from India and the United Kingdom. Iran had to turn to India for help in developing batteries that are reliable in the warm waters of the Gulf. Iran has also had problems with the air conditioning in the ships, and their serviceability has been erratic. There are serious questions about crew capability and readiness, and all three submarines already need significant refits.

Iran faces significant operational problems in using its submarines in local waters. Many areas of the Gulf do not favor submarine operations. The Gulf is about 241,000 square km in area, and it stretches 990 km from the Shatt al-Arab to the Strait of Hormuz. Its maximum width is about 340 km, and it is about 225 km wide for most of its length. Though heat patterns disturb surface sonar, they also disturb submarine sonar, and the advantage seems to be slightly in favor of sophisticated surface ships and maritime patrol aircraft.

The deeper parts of the Gulf are noisy enough to make ASW operations difficult, but large parts of the Gulf—including much of the Southern Gulf on a line from Al Jubail across the tip of Qatar to about half way up the United Arab Emirates—are less than 20 meters deep. The water is deeper on the Iranian side, but the maximum depth of the Gulf—located about 30 km south of Qeys Island—is still only 88 meters. This means that no point in the Gulf is deeper than the length of an SN-688 nuclear submarine. The keel-to-tower height of such a submarine alone is 16 meters. Even smaller coastal submarines have maneuver and bottom-suction problems, and they cannot hide in thermoclines or take advantage of diving for concealment or self-protection. This may explain why Iran is planning to relocate its submarines from Bandar Abbas, inside the Gulf, to Chah Bahar in the Gulf of Oman and is deepening the navy facility at Chah Bahar.[9]

The Strait of Hormuz at the entrance to the Gulf is about 180 km long, but it has a minimum width of 39 km, and only the two deepwater channels are suitable for major surface ship or submarine operations. Further, a limited flow of fresh water and a high evaporation rate make the Gulf extremely salty. This creates complex underwater currents in the main channels at the Strait of Hormuz and complicates both submarine operations and submarine detection. There are some areas with considerable noise, but not of a type that masks submarine noise from sophisticated ASW detection systems of the kind operated by the United States and United Kingdom. Further, the minimum operating depth of the Kilo is 45 meters, and the limited depth of the area around the strait can make submarine operations difficult. Submarines are easier to operate in the Gulf of Oman, which is noisy enough to make ASW operations difficult, but such deployments would expose the Kilos to operations by U.S. and British nuclear attack submarines. It is unlikely that Iran's Kilos could survive for any length of time if hunted by a U.S. or British navy air-surface-SSN (attack submarines) hunter-killer team.[10]

In any case, the effectiveness of Iran's submarines is likely to depend heavily on the degree of Western involvement in any ASW operation. If the Kilos did not face the U.S. or British ASW forces, the Iranian Kilos could operate in or near the Gulf with considerable impunity. If they did face U.S. and British forces, they might be able to attack a few tankers or conduct some mining efforts but would be unlikely to survive extended combat. This makes the Kilos a weapon that may be more effective in threatening Gulf shipping, or as a remote minelayer, than in naval combat. Certainly, Iran's purchase of the Kilos has already received close attention from the Southern Gulf states and convinced them that they must take Iran more seriously.

THE ROLE OF THE IRGC'S NAVAL BRANCH

Finally, any analysis of the capabilities of the Iranian Navy cannot ignore the fact that Iran's unconventional warfare capabilities include the naval branch of the IRGC, which operates Iran's land-based antiship missiles and coastal defense artillery. In addition to its land- and sea-based antiship missile forces, the naval guards can use large numbers of small patrol boats equipped with heavy machine guns, grenade launchers, antitank guided weapons, man-portable surface-to-air missiles, and 106 mm recoilless rifles.

The IRGC also uses small launches and at least 30 Zodiak rubber dinghies to practice rocket, small arms, and recoilless rifle attacks. Its other small craft are armed with a mix of machine guns, recoilless rifles, and man- and crew-portable antitank guided missiles. These vessels are difficult to detect by radar in anything but the calmest seas. Iran bases them at a number of offshore islands and oil platforms, and they can strike quickly and with limited warning. The naval branch of the IRGC also has naval artillery, divers, and mine-laying units. It had extensive stocks of Scuba equipment and an underwater combat center at Bandar Abbas.[11] Iran is also improving the defenses and port capabilities of its islands in the Gulf, adding covered moorings, more advanced sensors, and better air defenses.

Iran can use IRGC forces to conduct the kind of low-intensity or guerrilla warfare that can only be defeated by direct engagement with land forces, and filter substantial reinforcements into a coastal area on foot or with light vehicles, making such reinforcement difficult to attack. Iran can use virtually any surviving small craft to lay mines and to place unmoored mines in shipping lanes. Its IRGC forces can use small craft to attack offshore facilities and raid coastal targets. Finally, it is important to note that the United States did not successfully destroy a single land-based Iraqi antiship missile launcher during the Gulf War, and that the IRGC now has many dispersal launch sites and storage areas along a much longer coast. It also has a growing number of caves, shelters, and small hardened facilities. Such targets are sometimes difficult to detect until they are used, and they present added problems because they usually are too small and too numerous to attack with high-cost ordnance until it is clear that they have valuable enough contents to merit such an attack.

IRAN'S NAVAL FORCE DEPLOYMENTS

The main forces of the Iranian Navy are concentrated in the Gulf. Iran gives more importance to the security of its territorial sea in the Gulf area because in this direction it has highly complicated relations with various Arab nations, the United States, and Israel. Since the collapse of the Soviet Union, however, Iran's policy toward the Caspian Sea region has changed. According to the contracts between the Soviet Union and Iran, Tehran was not allowed to station its navy in the Caspian Sea. After the disintegration of the USSR, however, the 4th Naval Regional Forces started representing the Iranian Navy in the Caspian.[12]

Iran has almost 3,000 personnel in the Caspian. The forces include up to 50 fighting ships and support vessels, the Marine Corps, coastal guard forces, and the sea aircraft. There are also training vessels in the fleet, including one Shahrokh MSC minesweeper, two Hamzeh ships, and others. Currently, Iran has the second largest fleet in the Caspian after Russia. The fleet, however, is outdated. This is why Tehran has been trying to strengthen its naval forces in the Caspian through various programs. It is reported that the government has numerous plans to modernize its fleet. According to these projects, the future fleet will include several divisions and separate battalions of ships and submarines.[13]

IRAN'S OVERALL NAVAL CAPABILITIES

Iran's efforts have steadily improved its capabilities to threaten Gulf shipping and offshore oil facilities, its capability to support unconventional warfare, and its ability to defend Iran's offshore facilities, islands, and coastline. They have not, however, done much to help Iran to act as an effective "blue water" navy.

At the same time, the military capability of Iranian naval forces should not be measured in terms of Iran's ability to win a battle for sea control against U.S. and British naval forces, or any combination of Southern Gulf states supported by U.S. and British forces. For the foreseeable future, Iran's forces are likely to lose any such battle in a matter of days. As a result, it is Iran's ability to conduct limited or unconventional warfare, or to threaten traffic through the Gulf, that gives it the potential ability to threaten or intimidate its neighbors.

Notes

[1] *Jane's Sentinel Security Assessment: The Gulf States,* "Iran," October 29, 2001.

[2] *World Missiles Briefing,* Teal Group Corporation.

[3] *Jane's Defence Weekly,* June 25, 1997; Associated Press, June 17, 1997; United Press, June 17, 1997; *International Defense Review,* June 1996.

[4] *Jane's Fighting Ships, 2002–2003* (London: Jane's Information Group, 2003), 336–343.

[5] *Washington Times,* March 27, 1996.

[6] *Defense News,* January 17, 1994.

[7] *Jane's Fighting Ships, 2002–2003,* 336–343.

[8] Only two torpedo tubes can fire wire-guided torpedoes. *Defense News,* January 17, 1994.

[9] *Jane's Fighting Ships, 2002–2003,* 336–343.

[10] See David Miller, "Submarines in the Gulf," *Military Technology*, June 1993, 42–45; David Markov, "More Details Surface of Rubin's 'Kilo' Plans," *Jane's Intelligence Review*, May 1997, 209–215.

[11] In addition to the sources listed at the start of this section, these assessments are based on various interviews, various editions of International Institute for Strategic Studies, *The Military Balance* (London: International Institute for Strategic Studies, various years); the Jaffee Center for Strategic Studies, *The Middle East Military Balance* (Tel Aviv: Jaffee Center for Strategic Studies, various years); *Jane's Sentinel Security Assessment: The Gulf States,* "Iran," various editions; and *Jane's Defence Weekly,* July 11, 1987.

[12] A. Kozhikhov and D. Kaliyeva, "The Military Political Situation in the Caspian Region," *Central Asia's Affairs,* no: 3 (2002): 2–6.

[13] Ibid.

CHAPTER FIVE

THE IRANIAN AIR FORCE

The Iranian Air Force has some 52,000 men: 37,000 in the air force per se; and 15,000 in the Air Defense force, which operates Iran's land-based air defenses. It has more than 300 combat aircraft in its inventory (the International Institute for Strategic Studies estimates 306). Many of these aircraft, however, are either not operational or cannot be sustained in air combat. This includes 50 to 60 percent of Iran's U.S.- and French-supplied aircraft and some 20 to 30 percent of its Russian and Chinese supplied aircraft. It has 9 fighter ground attack squadrons with 162 to 186 aircraft; 7 fighter squadrons, with 70 to 74 aircraft; a reconnaissance unit with 4 to 8 aircraft; and a number of transport aircraft, helicopters, and special purpose aircraft. It operates most of Iraq's land-based air defenses, including some 150 I Hawks, 45 HQ-21s, 10 SA-5s, 30 Rapiers, and additional forces equipped with light surface-to-air missiles.

The Iranian air force is headquartered in Tehran, with training, administration, and logistics branches, as well as a major central Air Defense Operations Center. It has a political directorate and a small naval coordination staff. It has three major regional headquarters: the Northern Zone (Badl Sar), Central Zone (Hamaden), and Southern Zone (Bushehr). Each regional zone seems to control a major air defense sector with subordinate air bases and facilities. The key air defense subzones and related bases in the Northern Zone are at Badl Sar, Mashhad, and Shahabad Kord. The subzones and bases in the Central Zone are at Hamadan and Dezful, and the subzones and bases in the Southern Zone are at Bushehr, Bandar Abbas, and Jask. Iran has large combat air bases at Mehrabad, Tabriz, Hamadan, Dezful, Bushehr, Shiraz, Isfahan, and Bandar Abbas. It has smaller bases at least at 11 other locations. Shiraz provides interceptor training and is the main base for transport aircraft. Table 5.1 provides the details of the development of the force structure in the Iranian air force since the end of its war with Iraq in 1989, levels of labor power, and numbers and types of major weapons.

IRANIAN AIR STRENGTH

As is the case with most aspects of Iranian military forces, estimates differ by source. The International Institute for Strategic Studies estimates that the air force has 18 main combat squadrons. These include 9 fighter ground attack squadrons. Four squadrons have 55 to 65 U.S.-supplied F-4D/Es, 4 have 55 to 65 F-5E/FIIs, and 1 has 27 to 30 Soviet-supplied Su-24s. Iran had 7 Su-25K and 24 Mirage F-1 Iraqi aircraft that it seized during the Gulf War, and some may be operational. Some reports indicate that Iran has ordered an unknown number of TU-22M-3 "Backfire C" long-range strategic bombers from either Russia or Ukraine.[1] Discussions do seem to have taken place, but no deliveries or purchases can be confirmed.

Iran had seven air defense squadrons. Two squadrons had 20 to 25 U.S.-supplied F-14s, 2 had 25 to 30 Russian/Iraqi-supplied MiG-29s, and 1 had 25 to 35 Chinese supplied F-7Ms.[2] Finally, the Iranian air force had a small reconnaissance squadron with 3 to 8 RF-4Es. It has 5 C-130H MP maritime reconnaissance aircraft, 1 RC-130, and other intelligence/reconnaissance aircraft, together with large numbers of transports and helicopters.

Most Iranian squadrons can perform both air defense and attack missions, regardless of their principal mission—although this was not true of Iran's F-14 (air defense) and Su-24s (strike/attack) units. Iran's F-14s have not been able to use their Phoenix air-to-air missiles since the early 1980s. Iran has claimed that it is modernizing its F-14s by equipping them with I-Hawk missiles adapted to the air-to-air role, but it is far from clear that this is the case or that such adaptations can have more than limited effectiveness.[3]

Iran has made ambitious claims about aircraft production that it cannot as yet back up. Russian firms and the Iranian government tried to reach an agreement over license-production of the MiG-29, but repeated attempts have failed. Likely due to the difficulty the regime

Table 5.1
Iran's Air Force: Force Structure Trends, 1989– 2005

Aspect of Force Structure	1989–1990	1999–2000	2004–2005
Labor power	35,000	50,000	52,000
Air Force	?	25,000	37,000
Air Defense	?	25,000	15,000
Total combat aircraft	~121	304	306
Fighter ground attack	8/104	9/140	9/186
F-4D/E	35	50	65
F-5E/F	45	60	60
Su-24MK	0	30	30
Su-25K	0	0	7
CH J-6	24	0	0
Mirage F-1E	0	0	24
Fighter aircraft	1/15	7/110	7/74
F-14	15	60	25
F-7M	0	24	24
MiG-29A/UB	0	30	25
MR aircraft	2	0	5
P-3F	2	0	0
P-3MP	0	0	5
AEW aircraft	0	0	1
Il-76	0	0	1
RECCE aircraft	1/8	1/15	1/6
F-5	5	0	0
RF-4E	3	15	6
Tanker/transport aircraft	1/4	1/4	1/4
Boeing 707	4	3	3
Boeing 747	0	1	1
Transport aircraft	5/	5/47	5/60
Boeing 747F	9	6	4
Boeing 707	10	0	0
Boeing 727	0	1	1
C-130E/H	20	5	18
Commander 690	3	3	3
F-27	3	15	10
Falcon 20	9	4	1
Jetstar	0	1	2
PC-6B	0	10	10
Y-7	0	2	2
Il-76	0	0	?
Y-12(II)	0	0	9

(continued next page)

(Table 5.1, continued)

Aspect of Force Structure	1989–1990	1999–2000	2004–2005
Helicopters	51	46	34+
AB-206A	2	2	2
Bell 214C	39	39	30
Shabaviz 2061 / 2-75	0	0	?
CH-47	10	5	2
Training aircraft	84–85 (15)	134	151
Beech F-33A/C	26	26	20
EMB-312	5–6 (15)	15	15
PC-7	46	40	40
T-33	7	7	7
FT-7	0	5	15
F-5B	0	20	20
TB-21	0	8	8
TB-200	0	4	4
MiG-29B	0	5	0
MFI-17 Mushshaq	0	0	22
Air-to-surface missiles	0	?	3,000
AGM-65A Maverick	0	?	?
AS-10	0	?	?
AS-11	0	?	?
AS-14	0	?	?
C-801	0	?	?
Air-to-air missiles	?	?	?
AIM-7 Sparrow	?	?	?
AIM-9 Sidewinder	?	?	?
AIM-54 Phoenix	?	?	?
Surface-to-air missiles		200+	240+
I Hawk	105	100	150
Rapier	30	30	30
Tigercat	25	15	15
HQ-2J	50	45	45
SA-5	0	10	10
FM-80	0	?	?
SA-7	0	?	?
Stinger	0	?	?
AD Guns	0	0	?
23 mm: ZSU-23 Towed	0	0	?
37 mm: Oerlikon	0	0	?

Source: Adapted by Anthony H. Cordesman from International Institute for Strategic Studies, *The Military Balance* (London: International Institute for Strategic Studies, various years).

Note: (1) The number before the slash represent the number of squadrons, and the number after the slash represent the total number of aircraft. (2) A "?" means that the International Institute for Strategic Studies does not report the exact number, and a "+" means that number or greater.

has had in procuring new aircraft, Iran has been developing three new attack aircraft. The indigenous design and specifics of one of the fighters in development, the Shafagh, were unveiled at the Iran Airshow in 2002. Engineers hope to have a prototype by 2008, though it is unclear what the production numbers will be and what the real-world timetable for deployment may be.[4]

Little is known about the other two fighters in development, the Saeghe and the Azarakhsh, other than they have been reportedly derived from the F-5F. Claims have been made that the Azarakhsh is in low-rate production and has had operational weapons tests. There are also some indications that Iran is experimenting with composites in the Azarakhsh and is seeking to give it a locally modified beyond-visual-range radar for air-to-air combat.[5]

In practice, Iran is making light turboprop aircraft and a light utility helicopter. It is making enough progress so that it will probably be able to produce a jet trainer and heavier helicopters, but it is unclear how effective it can be in producing modern combat aircraft.[6]

Iran has moderate airlift capabilities for a regional power. The Iranian air force's air transport assets included 3 B-707 and 1 B-747 tanker transports, and 5 transport squadrons with 4 B-747Fs, 1 B-727, 18 C-130E/Hs, 3 Commander 690s, 10 F-27s, 1 Falcon 20A, and 2 Jetstars. Iran will have 14 Xian Y-7 transports by 2006.[7] Its helicopter strength includes 2 AB-206As; 27 to 30 Bell 214Cs; and 2 CH-47, 30 Mi-17 and Iranian-made Shabaviz 206-1, and 2 to 75 transport helicopters.

The Islamic Revolutionary Guards Corps (IRGC) also has some air elements. It is not clear what combat formations exist within the IRGC, but the IRGC may operate Iran's 10 EMB-312 Tucanos.[8] It seems to operate many of Iran's 45 PC-7 trainers, as well as some Pakistani-made trainers at a training school near Mushhak, but this school may be run by the regular air force. It has also claimed to manufacture gliders for use in unconventional warfare. The IRGC has not recently expanded its air combat capabilities.[9]

IRANIAN LAND-BASED AIR DEFENSE

Iran seems to have assigned about 12,000–15,000 men in its air force to land-based air defense functions, including at least 8,000 regulars and 4,000 IRGC personnel. It is not possible to distinguish clearly between the major air defense weapons holdings of the regular air force and IRGC, but the air force appeared to operate most major surface-to-air missile systems. Total holdings seem to include 30 Improved Hawk fire units (12 battalions / 150+ launchers), 45 to 55 SA-2 and HQ-2J/23 (CSA-1) launchers (Chinese-made equivalents of the SA-2), and possibly 25 SA-6 launchers. The air force also had three Soviet-made long-range SA-5 units with a total of 10 to 15 launchers—enough for six sites. Iran has developed and deployed its own domestically manufactured SAM, dubbed the Shahab Thaqeb. The SAM requires a four-wheeled trailer for deployment and closely resembles the R440 SAM.[10]

Iran's holdings of lighter air defense weapons include five Rapier squadrons with 30 Rapier fire units, 5 to 10 Chinese FM-80 launchers, 10 to 15 Tigercat fire units, and a few RBS-70s. Iran also holds large numbers of man-portable SA-7s, HN-5s, and SA-14s, plus about 2,000 antiaircraft guns—including some Vulcans and 50 to 60 radar-guided and self-propelled ZSU-23-4 weapons.[11] It is not clear which of these lighter air defense weapons were operated by the army, the IRGC, or the air force. The IRGC clearly had larger numbers of man-portable surface-to-air launchers, including some Stingers that it had obtained from Afghanistan. It almost certainly had a number of other light air defense guns as well.

There are no authoritative data on how Iran deploys air defenses, but Iran seems to have deployed its new SA-5s to cover its major ports, oil facilities, and Tehran. It seems to have concentrated its Improved Hawks and Soviet and Chinese-made SA-2s around Tehran, Isfahan, Shiraz, Bandar Abbas, Kharg Island, Bushehr, Bandar Khomeini, Ahwaz, Dezful, Kermanshah, Hamadan, and Tabriz. Iran's air defense forces are too widely spaced to provide more than limited air defense for key bases and facilities, and many lack the missile launcher strength to be fully effective. This is particularly true of Iran's SA-5 sites, which provide long-range, medium-to-high-altitude coverage of key coastal installations. Too few launchers are scattered over too wide an area to prevent relatively rapid suppression.

Iran also lacks the low-altitude radar coverage, overall radar net, command-and-control assets, sensors, resistance to sophisticated jamming and electronic countermeasures, and systems integration capability necessary to create an effective air defense net. Its land-based air defenses must operate largely in the point defense mode, and Iran lacks the battle management systems and its data links are not fast and effective enough to allow it to take maximum advantage of the overlapping coverage of some of its missile systems—a problem further complicated by the problems in trying to net different systems supplied by China, Russia, the United Kingdom, and the United States. Iran's missiles and sensors are most effective at high-to-medium altitudes against aircraft with limited penetrating and jamming capability.

IRANIAN AIR FORCE READINESS AND EFFECTIVENESS

In spite of Iran's efforts, readiness and force quality remain major issues. The Iranian air force still has many qualitative weaknesses, and it is far from clear that its current rate of modernization can offset the aging of its Western-supplied aircraft and the qualitative improvements in U.S. and Southern Gulf forces. The air force also faces serious problems in sustainment, command and control, and training. Iran has a pilot quality problem. Many of its U.S.-trained pilots were purged at some point during the Revolution. Its other U.S.-trained pilots and ground-crew technicians are aging to the point where many should soon retire from service and have not had advanced air-to-air combat and air attack training for more than 15 years.

Although Iran practices realistic individual intercept training, it fails to practice effective unit or force-wide tactics and has shown only limited capability to fly large numbers of sorties with its U.S.-supplied aircraft on even a surge basis. It has limited refueling capabilities—although it has four B-707 tanker/transports and may have converted other transports. The Iranian air force lacks advanced training facilities, and it has only limited capability to conduct realistic training for beyond-visual-range combat and standoff attacks with air-to-surface munitions. Ground crew training and proficiency generally seem mediocre—although the layout of Iranian air bases, aircraft storage, and parking; the deployment of equipment for maintenance cycles; and the other physical signs of air unit activity are generally better organized than those of most Middle Eastern air forces.

The Iranian air force must also deal with the fact that its primary challenge now consists of the U.S., British, and Saudi air forces. They are high-technology air forces that operate the airborne warning and control system, have some of the most advanced electronic warfare and targeting systems in the world, and have full refueling capability. They use sophisticated, computer-aided aggressor training and have all of the range and training facilities for beyond-visual-range combat and standoff attacks with air-to-surface munitions. Iran has no airborne control system, although it may be able to use the radar on its F-14s to support other aircraft from the rear. Its overall command, control, communications, computers, and intelligence (C^4I) system is a totally inadequate mix of different sensors, communications, and data-processing systems. It has limited electronic warfare capabilities by U.S. standards, although it may be seeking to acquire two Beriev A-50 Mainstay AEW aircraft and has converted some aircraft to provide a limited ELINT/SIGINT capability.

Iran is slowly improving its capability for joint land-air and air-sea operations. Iranian exercises and statements provide strong indications that Iran would like to develop an advanced air defense system, the ability to operate effectively in long-range maritime patrol and attack missions, effective joint warfare capabilities, and strike/attack forces with the ability to penetrate deep into Iraq, the Southern Gulf states, and other neighboring powers. Iran's exercises, military literature, and procurement efforts also make it clear that its air planners understand the value of airborne early warning and C^4I systems, the value of airborne intelligence and electronic warfare platforms, the value of remotely piloted vehicles, and the value of airborne refueling. Iran has even sought to create its own satellite program.[12] Further, the air force's efforts at sheltering and dispersal indicate that it understands the vulnerability of modern air facilities and the standoff attack capabilities of advanced air forces like those of the United States.

Notes

[1] *Jane's Sentinel Security Assessment: The Gulf States,* "Iran," October 7, 2004.

[2] The range of aircraft numbers shown reflects the broad uncertainties affecting the number of Iran's aircraft that are operational in any realistic sense. Many aircraft counted, however, cannot engage in sustained combat sorties in an extended air campaign. The numbers are drawn largely from interviews; *Jane's Intelligence Review,* Special Report 6, May 1995; *Jane's Sentinel Security Assessment: The Gulf States,* "Iran," various editions; International Institute for Strategic

Studies, *The Military Balance* (London: International Institute for Strategic Studies, various years), "Iran"; Andrew Rathmell, *The Changing Balance in the Gulf*, Whitehall Paper 38 (London: Royal United Services Institute, 1996); Andrew Rathmell, "Iran's Rearmament: How Great a Threat?" *Jane's Intelligence Review*, July 1994, 317–322; *Jane's World Air Forces*, CD-ROM.

[3] *Wall Street Journal*, February 10, 1995; *Washington Times*, February 10, 1995.

[4] *Jane's All the World's Aircraft, 2002–2003* (London: Jane's Information Group), 259–263.

[5] Robert Hewson, "Iran's New Combat Aircraft Waits in the Wings," *Jane's Defence Weekly*, November 20, 2002. *Jane's All the World's Aircraft, 2002–2003*, 259–263.

[6] *Jane's All the World's Aircraft, 2002–2003*, 259–263.

[7] Periscope, Nations / Alliances / Geographic Regions / Middle East / North Africa, Plans and Programs.

[8] Reports that the IRGC is operating F-7 fighters do not seem to be correct.

[9] Reuters, June 12, 1996.

[10] "Iran Reveals Shahab Thaqeb SAM Details," *Jane's Defence Weekly*, September 4, 2002.

[11] This is based on interviews with British, Israeli, and U.S. experts; and on Anthony H. Cordesman, *Iran and Iraq: The Threat from the Northern Gulf* (Boulder, Colo.: Westview Press, 1994); Anthony H. Cordesman and Ahmed S. Hashim, *Iran: The Dilemmas of Dual Containment* (Boulder, Colo.: Westview Press, 1997); International Institute for Strategic Studies, *Military Balance*, various editions, "Iran"; *Jane's Sentinel Security Assessment: The Gulf States*, various editions, "Iran"; U.S. Naval Institute Data Base; Anoushiravan Ehteshami, "Iran's National Strategy," *International Defense Review*, April 1994, 29–37; Military Technology, *World Defense Almanac: The Balance of Military Power* 17, issue 1 (1993): 139–142; working data from the Jaffee Center for Strategic Studies; Rathmell, "Iran's Rearmament"; Ahmed Hashim, *The Crisis of the Iranian State*, Adelphi Paper 296 (London: International Institute for Strategic Studies, 1995), 7–30, 50–70; Rathmell, *Changing Military Balance in the Gulf*, 9–23; Michael Eisenstadt, *Iranian Military Power, Capabilities and Intentions* (Washington, D.C.: Washington Institute, 1996), 9–65; and Anoushiravan Enreshami, "Iran Strives to Regain Military Might," *International Defense Review*, July 1996, 22–26.

[12] *Jane's Defence Weekly*, September 4, 1996.

CHAPTER SIX

IRANIAN CAPABILITIES TO CARRY OUT ATTACKS IN THE GULF

The conventional military threat from Iran may be limited, but it could still launch asymmetric attacks in the Gulf that would have a strategic effect out of proportion to the size and capability of its forces. Iran is a potential threat to shipping in the Gulf as well as in the Gulf of Oman. It can also attack targets throughout the Gulf Coast, and the Gulf contains 715 billion barrels of proven oil reserves, representing more than half (57 percent) of the world's oil reserves, and 2,462 trillion cubic feet of natural gas reserves (45 percent of the world total). Saudi Arabia alone has more than 20 percent of the world's proven oil reserves, and Saudi Arabia exported some 49 percent of Gulf exports in 2003.[1]

THE STRAIT OF HORMUZ AND GULF SHIPPING CHANNELS

Iran's territory includes the northern coast of the Strait of Hormuz and the coast on either side. Oman occupies the islands in the strait, and Goat Island and the Musandam Peninsula to the south. The strait is the world's most important oil chokepoint. As noted above, it is 180 kilometers long and 39 kilometers wide at its narrowest passage. The strait has channels for inbound and outbound tanker traffic that are only 2 miles wide, plus a 2-mile-wide buffer zone. Some 40 percent of all world oil exports (15–15.5 million barrels per day, or mmbpd) now pass daily through the Strait of Hormuz, the entrance to the Gulf from the Gulf of Oman and the Indian Ocean. Projections by the U.S. Energy Information Administraion (EIA) and the International Energy Agency (IEA) indicate that this total will increase to about 60 percent by 2025 to 2030.[2]

Iran has serious vulnerabilities of its own, but this does not mean there is any guarantee that it would not attack Saudi or other Gulf facilities. As discussed above, Iran occupies a number of islands in the main shipping channels to the Strait of Hormuz on the Gulf side. These include the Tunbs, Abu Musa, Qeshem, Larak, Hormuz, Sirri, and Bani Forur. It has a major naval and air base on the coast above the strait at Bandar Abbas.

Abu Musa and the Greater and Lesser Tunb Islands present special problems because they are located in the main shipping channels just to the west of the Strait of Hormuz. They are disputed territory between Iran and the United Arab Emirates that Iranian troops seized in 1992. The Iranian Foreign Ministry claimed that the islands are "an inseparable part of Iran" in 1965, and Iran rejected a proposal by the Gulf Cooperation Council in 1996 to have the International Court of Justice resolve the dispute. It has since strengthened is presence in the islands by starting up a power plant on Greater Tunb and opening an airport on Abu Musa. It has said that it will construct a new port on Abu Musa.[3]

Although Iran has not fortified the islands in the shipping channels, it has deployed the Islamic Revolutionary Guards Corps to some of these islands, and a number have airfields or airstrips and limited naval facilities. It is within a few minutes flight time of the Strait of Hormuz, and it has other bases on the Gulf Coast extending to locations near its border with Kuwait. It is within 5 to 7 minutes flight time of targets on the coast of Saudi Arabia and the Gulf Coast of every other Southern Gulf state, and its mountains make a natural radar shield for "pop up" air attacks with limited warning unless an airborne warning and control system is patrolling in the area. The Islamic Revolutionary Guards Corps and Iranian naval forces can deploy to the shipping channels and Saudi waters in a matter of hours, and Iran showed during the Iran-Iraq War that it could deploy free-floating mines in the shipping channels in ways that were very difficult to detect. Iran can also attack shipping in the Strait of Hormuz and the Gulf of Oman.

THE GULF COAST AND KEY FACILITIES

Saudi Arabia and the other Gulf states have substantial vulnerabilities to attacks on shipping inside the Gulf, on its tanker-loading facilities, and on power and desalination plants along the Gulf Coast. Though vulnerability studies often focus on petroleum exports, the Gulf states are acutely vulnerable to attacks on their water and power facilities. Saudi Arabia alone gets 60 percent of its water from some 30 desalination plants with a capacity of 3.4 million cubic meters a day, although many are on its Red Sea coast.[4] Virtually all future increase in Gulf water use must come from such desalination plants, and output must rise at an average rate of at least 3 percent a year for the foreseeable future. Saudi Arabia, for example, plans to increase capacity to 4.4 million cubic meters a day by 2010 and 5.5 million cubic meters a day by 2020. [5]

There are many major offshore oil facilities, including Safaniya (the world's largest offshore oil field, with estimated reserves of 35 billion barrels). The EIA reports that Saudi offshore production includes Arab Medium Crude from the Zuluf (more than 500,000 mmbpd capacity) and Marjan (270,000 mmbpd capacity) fields and Arab Heavy Crude from the Safaniya field.

Saudi Arabia shares the Neutral Zone with Kuwait, which contains about 5 billion barrels of proven oil reserves and has two offshore fields (Khafji and Hout) producing some 300,000 mmbpd. There is also a large natural gas field, called Dorra, located offshore near the Khafji oil field. The development of this field presents problems because it is also claimed by Iran (which calls the field Arash). Saudi Arabia did reach an agreement with Kuwait to share Dorra equally in July 2000, but the maritime border between Kuwait and Iran remains undemarcated. Iran and Kuwait have held boundary discussions since 2000, but Iran continues to oppose Saudi and Kuwaiti efforts to develop the field.[6]

SAUDI EXPORT FACILITIES

The EIA provides the following description of Saudi oil export facilities and its overall dependence on the security of the Gulf and access through the Strait of Hormuz:[7]

Most of Saudi Arabia's crude oil is exported from the Persian Gulf via the huge Abqaiq processing facility, which handles around two-thirds or so of the country's oil output. Saudi Arabia's primary oil export terminals are located at Ras Tanura (6 million bbl/d [barrels per day] capacity; the world's largest offshore oil loading facility) and Ras al-Ju'aymah (3 million bbl/d) on the Persian Gulf, plus Yanbu (as high as 5 million bbl/d) on the Red Sea. Combined, these terminals appear capable of handling around 14 million bbl/d, around 3.5-4.0 million bbl/d higher than Saudi crude oil production capacity (10–10.5 million bbl/d), and about 6 million bbl/d in excess of Saudi crude oil production in 2002. Despite this excess capacity, there have been reports that the Saudis are planning to conduct a feasibility study on construction of an oil pipeline from the Empty Quarter of southeastern Saudi Arabia through the Hadramaut in Yemen to the Arabian Sea.

Saudi Arabia operates two major oil pipelines. The 5 million bbl/d East–West Crude Oil Pipeline (Petroline), operated by Aramco since 1984 (when it took over from Mobil), is used mainly to transport Arabian Light and Super Light to refineries in the Western Province and to Red Sea terminals for export to European markets. The Petroline was constructed in 1981, with initial capacity of 1.85 million bbl/d on a single, 48-inch line (AY-1). The Petroline was expanded in 1987, during the height of the Iran-Iraq war (and specifically the so-called "tanker war" in the Gulf), to 3.2 million bbl/d, with the addition of a parallel ("looped"), 56-inch line (AY-1L). Finally, in 1993, Petroline capacity was increased to 5.0 million bbl/d by adding significant pumping capability on the line. Reportedly, the Saudis expanded the Petroline in part to maintain Yanbu as a strategic option to Gulf port facilities in the event that exports were blocked at that end. A study in 1997 by the Baker Institute indicated that capacity on the Petroline could be expanded significantly by using so-called "drag reduction agents" (DRAs), and that this could enhance the line's strategic value.

In purely economic terms, Yanbu remains a far less economical option for Saudi oil exports than Ras Tanura. Among other factors, shipments from Yanbu add about 5 days roundtrip travel time for tankers through the Bab al-Mandab strait to major customers in Asia compared to Ras Tanura (via the Strait of Hormuz). In addition, according to Oil Minister Naimi, the Petroline is only utilized at half capacity. Given this fact, as well as the desire to boost natural gas usage (see below), Saudi Aramco has begun converting the AY-1 (48-inch) line to natural gas pumping capability. The natural gas will supply Yanbu's petrochemical and power facilities.

Running parallel to the Petroline is the 290,000 bbl/d Abqaiq-Yanbu natural gas liquids pipeline, which serves Yanbu's petrochemical plants. The Trans-Arabian Pipeline (Tapline) to Lebanon is mothballed, and the 1.65-million-bbl/d, 48-inch Iraqi Pipeline across Saudi Arabia (IPSA), which runs parallel to the Petroline from pump station #3 (there are 11 pumping stations along the Petroline, all utilizing on-site gas turbine electric generators) to the port of Mu'ajjiz, just south of Yanbu, was closed indefinitely following the August 1990 Iraqi invasion of Kuwait (also, in June 2001, Saudi Arabia seized ownership of IPSA "in light of the Iraqi government's persistence in its stands"). Theoretically, IPSA could be used for Saudi oil transport to the Red Sea, although the Saudis have stated that "there are no plans" to do so. According to Oil Minister Naimi, Saudi Arabia has "surplus oil export and pipelines capacity. . . [including the] East-West oil pipeline system [which] can carry and deliver 5 million bbl/d" but is being run at "only half capacity."

. . . SABIC, the Middle East's largest non-oil industrial company (and expected to become one of the world's top five ethylene producers by 2005), accounts for around 10% of world petrochemical production. In February 2001, SABIC completed a $1 billion expansion at the Yanbu petrochemical facility, making it the largest polyethylene plant in the world. . . . In early January 2002, SABIC agreed to a $1.15 billion loan to fund a new petrochemicals plant in the eastern Saudi Arabian industrial city of Jubail. The complex is scheduled to come online in the second half of 2004, and to produce 1 million tons per year of ethylene, plus olefins, polyethylene, and glycol ethylene.

. . . Aramco's shipping subsidiary Vela has the world's largest fleet of oil tankers, including 19 VLCC's (very large crude carriers) and 4 ULCC's (ultra large crude carriers). Overall, Vela carries around half of Saudi oil exports. In addition to tankers, Aramco owns or leases oil storage facilities around the world, in places like Rotterdam, Sidi Kerir (the Sumed pipeline terminal on Egypt's Mediterranean coast), South Korea, the Philippines, the Caribbean, and the United States.

INCREASING GLOBAL DEPENDENCE ON GULF EXPORTS

To put this situation in broader perspective, the security of the Gulf and exports from the Gulf are critical to both Saudi Arabia and all the world's oil importers. Moreover, global dependence on such exports will increase steadily with time. Projections by the IEA indicate that Middle Eastern exports will total some 46 mmbpd by 2030 and represent more that two-thirds of the world total.

This means that the daily traffic in oil tankers will increase from 15 mmbpd and 44 percent of global interregional trade in 2002 to 43 mmbpd and 66 percent of global interregional trade in 2030. The daily traffic in liquefied natural gas carriers will increase from 28 billion cubic meters and 18 percent of global interregional trade in 2002 to 230 carriers and 34 percent of global interregional trade in 2030.[8]

The IEA also estimates that imports will rise from 63 percent of total demand for oil in 2002 by the countries belonging to the Organization for Economic Cooperation and Development to 85 percent in 2030. Therefore, some $3 trillion dollars must be invested in the oil sector from 2003 to 2030 to meet world demand for oil, and something approaching half of this total must be invested in the Middle East and North Africa. Some $234 billion will be required for tankers and oil pipelines, and again, a substantial amount must go to the Middle East and North Africa.[9]

Notes

[1] U.S. Energy Information Administration (EIA), "Persian Gulf Fact Sheet," September 2004, http://www.eia.doe.gov/emeu/cabs/pgulf.html.

[2] See http://www.eia.doe.gov/emeu/security/choke.html#HORMUZ. The Strait of Hormuz is the narrow passage between Iran and Oman that connects the Persian Gulf with the Gulf of Oman and the Arabian Sea. It consists of 2-mile-wide channels for inbound and outbound tanker traffic, as well as a 2-mile-wide buffer zone. The EIA estimates that some 13 mmbpd flowed through the Strait in 2002. The IEA puts the figure at 15 mmbpd in 2003. Both agencies indicate that the amount of oil moving by tanker will increase steadily as Asian demand consumes a larger and larger share of total exports.

Closure of the Strait of Hormuz would require use of longer alternate routes (if available) at increased transportation costs. Such routes include the 5 mmbpd capacity Petroline (East-West Pipeline) and the 290,000 mmbpd Abqaiq-Yanbu natural gas liquids line across Saudi Arabia to the Red Sea. Theoretically, the 1.65 mmbpd Iraqi Pipeline across Saudi Arabia (IPSA) also could be utilized, more oil could be pumped north to Ceyhan (Turkey), and the 0.5 mmbpd Tapline to Lebanon could be reactivated.

[3] EIA, "UAE Country Brief," February 2004, http://www.eia.doe.gov/emeu/cabs/uae.html.

[4] *Arab News*, December 6, 2004; *Middle East Economic Digest*, November 12–18, 2004.

[5] *Middle East Economic Digest*, November 12–18, 2004.

[6] EIA, "Saudi Country Brief," June 2004, http://www.eia.doe.gov/emeu/cabs/saudi.html.

[7] This is from http://www.eia.doe.gov/emeu/cabs/saudi.html.

[8] IEA, "Oil Market Outlook," in *World Energy Outlook, 2004* (Paris: Organization for Economic Cooperation and Development and IEA, 2004), chap. 3, tables 3.7 and 3.8.

[9] IEA, "Oil Market Outlook."

CHAPTER SEVEN

IRANIAN PROLIFERATION AND WEAPONS OF MASS DESTRUCTION

Iran has many reasons for acquiring weapons of mass destruction, although it has never openly declared its intentions or admitted to a nuclear weapons program. This makes it impossible to determine Iran's precise motives and intentions, but it is seems likely that they include a mix of the following factors:

- A defensive political ruling elite that has survived the Iran-Iraq War, lost the "tanker war" of 1987–1988 to the United States, and seen the impact of U.S. conventional superiority in the Gulf War of 1991 and the Iraqi War of 2003.

- U.S. policy-level discussions of regime overthrow in Iran; attacks on Iran for its support of Hizballah, Hamas, and other enemies of Israel; preemptive strikes on Iran's nuclear facilities; and President George W. Bush's description of Iran as part of the "axis of evil."

- Iran's problems in modernizing its conventional forces.

- The legacy of the shah's ambitious efforts to make Iran a major military power and the high probability that he started and maintained a covert nuclear weapons program.

- The legacy of the Iran-Iraq War and Iraq's extensive use of chemical weapons against Iran, plus its use of conventionally armed ballistic missiles against Iranian cities.

- The legacy of the Gulf War, and the lesson that Iraq could use missiles against targets in Saudi Arabia and Israel.

- The broad lesson that weak conventional forces cannot deter or defend against the United States.

- The potential threat posed by a hostile Israel, with its own long-range strike systems and nuclear weapons.
- The example set by nations like India, Pakistan, and North Korea.
- The fact that nuclear weapons provide a unique level of military status and prestige, and could potentially make Iran something approaching a regional superpower.
- The potential ability to use long-range missiles and the possession of nuclear weapons not only to deter the United States and Iran's neighbors but also to intimidate and pressure Iran's neighbors to support its policies and/or to deter interference in limited Iranian military operations in areas like Iraq or the Gulf.
- A belief that Iran must be able to retaliate against any U.S. or regional attack that threatens its regime or the defeat of its conventional forces.

It should be noted that it is impossible to determine what combination of these motives will drive Iran's behavior, and it is dangerous to assume that Iran has fixed plans for proliferation or the use of the forces it develops. Iran faces so much opposition to acquiring such weapons that it is forced to proliferate on a target-of-opportunity basis and to constantly adapt its approaches to acquiring weapons and delivery systems. Even if it has force plans, it will almost certainly change them over time—and necessarily its doctrine, war plans, and targeting.

It is also extremely dangerous to assume that Iran would actually behave in a war or crisis as if it were a perfect "rational bargainer." Iran has not acted aggressively in the past in military terms, and its ruling elite has been cautious in taking risks. History provides warning after warning, however, that behavior can change radically, and take unpredictable risks, in the face of a major crisis. The history of the West in the twentieth century is filled with such examples and is ample proof that this takes place regardless of nation and culture.

As for Iran's current efforts, its missile developments have already been discussed. In terms of Iran's efforts to acquire weapons of mass destruction, the country has declared that it has the capacity to make chemical weapons. The details of its biological warfare efforts are unknown, but it continues to import suspect biotechnology. It is also moving forward in the nuclear dimension. The International Atomic

Energy Agency (IAEA) has discovered a number of disturbing details about its uranium enrichment program that are similar to Libya's nuclear weapons program, including the ability to produce P-2 centrifuges. Iran has conducted experiments with uranium hexafluoride that could fuel a weapons oriented enrichment program, and it has worked on a heavy water plant that could be used in a reactor design that would produce fissile material far more efficiently than its Russian-supplied light water reactor.

Although it is not yet confirmed, Iran may well have received the same older Chinese design data for a nuclear weapon of 1,000 to 2,000 pounds that Libya acquired through Pakistani sources. U.S. secretary of state Colin Powell declared on November 17, 2004, that Iran was preparing its missiles to carry nuclear weapons, although he did not provide details.[1] The United States also announced the next day that Iran was rushing its processing of uranium hexafluoride forward to complete the processing before its negotiations with Europe might force it to halt.

THE STATUS OF THE IRANIAN CHEMICAL WEAPONS PROGRAM

Iran has pursued chemical weapons since at least the time it first came under Iraqi chemical attack early in the Iran-Iraq War. It purchased large amounts of chemical defense gear from the mid-1980s onward. Iran also obtained stocks of nonlethal CS gas, although it quickly found such agents had very limited military impact because they could only be used effectively in closed areas or very small open areas. Acquiring poisonous chemical agents was more difficult. Iran did not have any internal capacity to manufacture poisonous chemical agents when Iraq first launched its attacks with such weapons. Though Iran seems to have made limited use of chemical mortar and artillery rounds as early as 1985—and possibly as early as 1984—these rounds were almost certainly captured from Iraq.

Iran had to covertly import the necessary equipment and supplies, and it took several years to get substantial amounts of production equipment and the necessary feedstocks. Iran sought aid from European firms like Lurgi to produce large "pesticide" plants, and it began to try to obtain the needed feedstock from a wide range of sources, relying heavily on its embassy in Bonn to manage the necessary deals. Though Lurgi did not provide the pesticide plant Iran sought, Iran did obtain substantial support from other European firms and feedstocks from many other Western sources.

By the period 1986–1987, Iran had developed the capability to produce enough lethal agents to load its own weapons. The director of the U.S. Central Intelligence Agency, along with informed observers in the Gulf, made it clear that Iran could produce blood agents like hydrogen cyanide, phosgene gas, and/or chlorine gas. Iran was also able to weaponize limited quantities of blister (sulfur mustard) and blood (cyanide) agents beginning in 1987, and it had some capability to weaponize phosgene gas and/or chlorine gas. These chemical agents were produced in small batches, and evidently under laboratory scale conditions, which enabled Iran to load small numbers of weapons before any of its new major production plants went into full operation. These gas agents were loaded into bombs and artillery shells, and they were used sporadically against Iraq in 1987 and 1988.

Reports regarding Iran's production and research facilities since that time are highly uncertain:

- Iran seems to have completed a major poison gas plant at Qazvin, about 150 kilometers west of Tehran. This plant is reported to have been completed between November 1987 and January 1988. Though supposedly a pesticide plant, the facility's true purpose seems to have been poison gas production using organophosphorous compounds.

- It is impossible to trace all the sources of the major components and technology Iran used in its chemical weapons program during this period. Mujahideen sources claim Iran also set up a chemical bomb and warhead plant operated by the Zakaria Al-Razi chemical company near Mahshar in southern Iran, but it is unclear whether these reports are true.

- Reports that Iran had chemical weapons plants at Damghan and Parchin that began operation as early as March 1988, and may have begun to test fire Scuds with chemical warheads as early as 1988–1989, are equally uncertain.

- Iran established at least one large research and development center under the control of the Engineering Research Centre of the

Construction Crusade (Jahad e-Sazandegi), and it had established a significant chemical weapons production capability by mid-1989.

- Debates took place in the Iranian parliament, the Majlis, in late 1988 over the safety of Pasdaran gas plants located near Iranian towns, and that President Hashemi Rafsanjani described chemical weapons as follows: "Chemical and biological weapons are poor man's atomic bombs and can easily be produced. We should at least consider them for our defense. Although the use of such weapons is inhuman, the war taught us that international laws are only scraps of paper."

The estimates of Iran's chemical weapons production that were made after the Iran-Iraq War are largely speculative:

- U.S. experts believe Iran was beginning to produce significant mustard gas and nerve gas by the time of the August 1988 cease-fire in the Iran-Iraq War, although its use of chemical weapons remained limited and had little impact on the fighting.

- Iran's efforts to equip plants to produce V-agent nerve gases seem to have been delayed by U.S., British, and German efforts to limit technology transfers to Iran, but Iran may have acquired the capability to produce persistent nerve gas during the mid-1990s.

- Production of nerve gas weapons started no later than 1994.

- Iran began to stockpile of cyanide (cyanogen chloride), phosgene, and mustard gas weapons after 1985. Recent CIA testimony indicates that Iran's production capacity may approach 1,000 tons annually.

- On August 2, 2002, the National Security Council's director for the Near East indicated that Iran is producing and stockpiling blister, blood, and choking agents.

- The Defense Department's 2001 report "Proliferation: Threat and Response" suggests that Iran, in addition to producing and stockpiling blister, blood, and choking agents, has weaponized these agents for use with artillery shells, mortars, rockets, and bombs. The report also states that Iran is continuing its research into nerve agents.

- Weapons include bombs and artillery. Shells include 155 millimeter artillery and mortar rounds. Iran also has chemical bombs and mines. It may have developmental chemical warheads for its Scuds, and it may have a chemical package for its 22006 remotely piloted vehicle (doubtful).

- There are reports that Iran has deployed chemical weapons on some of its ships. Training for Iranian naval forces suggests that they are preparing for the possibility of operating in a contaminated environment.
- Iran has increased its chemical defensive and offensive warfare training since 1993.

Iran has sought to buy more advanced chemical defense equipment, and it also has sought to buy specialized equipment on the world market to develop an indigenous capability to produce advanced feedstocks for nerve weapons:

- CIA sources indicated in late 1996 that China might have supplied Iran with up to 400 tons of chemicals for the production of nerve gas.
- One report indicated in 1996 that Iran obtained 400 metric tons of chemicals for use in nerve gas weapons from China—including carbon sulfide.
- Another report indicated that China had supplied Iran with roughly 2 tons of calcium hypochlorate in 1996 and had loaded another 40,000 barrels in January or February 1997. Calcium hypochlorate is used for decontamination in chemical warfare (CW).
- Iran placed several significant orders from China that were not delivered. Razak Industries in Tehran and Chemical and Pharmaceutical Industries in Tabriz ordered 49 metric tons of alkyl dimethylamine, a chemical used in making detergents, and 17 tons of sodium sulfide, a chemical used in making mustard gas. The orders were never delivered, but they were brokered by Iran's International Movalled Industries Corporation (Imaco) and China's North Chemical Industries Company (Nocinco). Both brokers have been linked to other transactions affecting Iran's chemical weapons program since early 1995, and Nocinco has supplied Iran with several hundred tons of carbon disulfide, a chemical used in nerve gas.
- Another Chinese firm, publicly only identified as Q. Chen, seems to have supplied glass vessels for chemical weapons.

■ The United States imposed sanctions on seven Chinese firms in May 1997 for selling precursors for nerve gas and equipment for making nerve gas—although the United States made it clear that it had "no evidence that the Chinese government was involved." The Chinese firms were the Nanjing Chemical Industries Group and Jiangsu Yongli Chemical Engineering and Import/Export Corporation. Cheong Yee Limited, a Hong Kong firm, was also involved. The precursors included thionyl chloride, dimethylamine, and ethylene chlorohydril. The equipment included special glass-lined vessels, and Nanjing Chemical and Industrial Group completed the construction of a production plant to manufacture these vessels in Iran in June 1997.

■ Iran sought to obtain impregnated alumina, which is used to make phosphorous oxychloride—a major component of the poison gases VX and GB (sarin)—from the United States.

■ Iran has obtained some equipment from Israelis. Nahum Manbar, an Israeli national living in France, was convicted in an Israeli court in May 1997 for providing Iran with $16 million worth of production equipment for mustard and nerve gas during the period from 1990 to 1995.

■ The CIA reported in June 1997 that Iran had obtained new chemical weapons equipment technology from China and India in 1996.

■ India is assisting in the construction of a major new plant at Qazvim, near Tehran, to manufacture phosphorous pentasulfide, a major precursor for nerve gas. The plant is fronted by Meli Agrochemicals, and the program was negotiated by Mejid Tehrani Abbaspour, a chief security adviser to President Rafsanjani.

■ A number of reports indicate that China has provided Iran with the ability to manufacture chemical weapons indigenously as well as providing precursors since at least 1996.[2]

■ A recent report by German intelligence indicates that Iran has made major efforts to acquire the equipment necessary to produce Sarin and Tabun, using the same cover of purchasing equipment for pesticide plants that Iraq used for its Sa'ad 16 plant in the 1980s. German sources note that three Indian companies— Tata Consulting Engineering, Transpek, and Rallis India—have approached German pharmaceutical and engineering concerns for this equipment and technology under conditions whereby German intelligence was able to trace the end user to Iran.

Iran ratified the Chemical Weapons Convention (CWC) in June 1997, but it is far from clear what this means. It submitted a statement in Farsi to the CWC secretariat in 1998, but this consisted only of questions as to the nature of the required compliance. It has not provided the CWC with detailed data on its chemical weapons program. Iran also stridently asserted its right to withdraw from the CWC at any time. Related events include the following:

- The CIA stated that Chinese entities sought to supply Iran with CW-related chemicals during 1997–1998 period. The U.S. sanctions imposed in May 1997 on seven Chinese entities for knowingly and materially contributing to Iran's CW program remain in effect.

- The CIA estimated in January 1999 that Iran had obtained material related to CW from various sources during the first half of 1998. It already has manufactured and stockpiled chemical weapons, including blister, blood, and choking agents and the bombs and artillery shells for delivering them. However, Tehran is seeking foreign equipment and expertise to create a more advanced and self-sufficient CW infrastructure.

- On May 2, 2003, the Iranian news agency, IRNA, issued a report stating that Iran called "on all world countries to take serious and coordinated measures to obliterate chemical weapons."

- In mid-May 2003, the Bush administration released a statement to the Organization for Prohibition of Chemical Weapons in which the United States accused Iran of continuing to pursue production technology, training, and expertise from abroad. The statement asserts that Iran is continuing to stockpile blister, blood, choking, and some nerve agents.

- The CIA reported in November 2003 that "Iran is a party to the CWC. Nevertheless, during the reporting period, it continued to seek production technology, training, and expertise from Chinese entities that could further Tehran's efforts to achieve an indigenous capability to produce nerve agents. Iran likely has already stockpiled blister, blood, choking, and probably nerve agents—and the bombs and artillery shells to deliver them— which it previously had manufactured."

A number of sites in Iran are alleged to be related to Iran's chemical warfare effort:[3]

- Abu Musa Island: Iran holds a large number of chemical weapons, principally 155 millimeter artillery shells, in addition to some weaponized biological agents.

- Bandar Khomeni: Allegedly the location of a chemical weapons facility, run by the Razi chemical corporation, established during the Iran-Iraq War to manufacture chemical weapons.

- Damghan: Either a chemical weapons plant or warhead assembly facility. Primarily involved in 155 millimeter artillery shells and SCUD warheads.

- Esfahan: Suspected location of a chemical weapons facility, possibly operated by the Poly-Acryl Corporation.

- Karaj: Located about 14 kilometers from Tehran, this is the site of an alleged storage and manufacturing facility for chemical weapons. Reports suggest that this facility was built with Chinese assistance.

- Marvdasht: The Chemical Fertilizers Company is suspected to have been a manufacturing facility for mustard agents during the Iran-Iraq War.

- Parchin: This is the location of at least one munitions factory and is suspected of being a major chemical weapons production facility. Reports of uncertain reliability indicate that the plant was in operation no later than March 1988. In April 1997, a German newspaper reported that, according to the German Federal Intelligence Service, the factories at Parchin were producing primary products for chemical warfare agents.

- Qazvin: A large pesticide plant at this location is widely believed to produce nerve gas.

- Mashar: Iranian opposition groups have made allegations, of uncertain reliability, that a warhead-filling facility is operated at this location.

It seems likely that Iran retains some chemical weapons and could employ them in combat. It does not, however, overtly train for offensive chemical warfare, and its current and future war fighting capabilities are unknown.

THE STATUS OF THE IRANIAN BIOLOGICAL
WEAPONS PROGRAM

Any analysis of Iran's biological weapons effort must be even more speculative. Iran does have both an extensive laboratory and research capability and steadily improving industrial facilities with dual-use production capabilities. Whether it has an active weapons development program, however, is a controversial matter.

Reports first surfaced in 1982—during the Iran-Iraq War—that Iran had imported suitable cultures from Europe and was working on the production of mycotoxins—a relatively simple family of biological agents that require only limited laboratory facilities for small-scale production. Many experts believe that the Iranian biological weapons effort was placed under the control of the Islamic Revolutionary Guards Corps (IRGC), which is known to have tried to purchase suitable production equipment for such weapons.

U.S. intelligence sources reported in August 1989 that Iran was trying to buy two new strains of fungus from Canada and the Netherlands that can be used to produce mycotoxins. German sources indicated that Iran had successfully purchased such cultures several years earlier. Some universities and research centers may be linked to Iran's biological weapons program. The Imam Reza Medical Center at Mashhad Medical Sciences University and the Iranian Research Organization for Science and Technology were identified as the end users for this purchasing effort, but it is likely that the true end user was an Iranian government agency specializing in biological warfare.

Since the Iran-Iraq War, Iran may have conducted research on more lethal active agents like Anthrax, hoof and mouth disease, and biotoxins. Iranian groups have repeatedly approached various European firms for equipment and technology that could be used to work with these diseases and toxins.

Unclassified sources of uncertain reliability have identified a facility at Damghan as working on both biological and chemical weapons research and production, and believe that Iran may be producing biological weapons at a pesticide facility near Tehran.

Reports surfaced in the spring of 1993 that Iran had succeeded in obtaining advanced biological weapons technology in Switzerland and containment equipment and technology from Germany. According to these reports, this led to serious damage to computer facilities in a Swiss biological research facility by unidentified agents. Similar reports indicated that agents had destroyed German biocontainment equipment destined for Iran. More credible reports by U.S. experts indicate that Iran might have begun to stockpile anthrax and Botulinum in a facility near Tabriz, can now mass-manufacture such agents, and has them in an aerosol form. None of these reports, however, can be verified.

The CIA has reported that Iran has "sought dual-use biotech equipment from Europe and Asia, ostensibly for civilian use." It also reported in 1996 that Iran might be ready to deploy biological weapons. Beyond this point, little unclassified information exists regarding the details of Iran's effort to "weaponize" and produce biological weapons.

The CIA reported in 1996 that "we believe that Iran holds some stocks of biological agents and weapons. Tehran probably has investigated both toxins and live organisms as biological warfare agents. Iran has the technical infrastructure to support a significant biological weapons program with little foreign assistance."

Iran announced in June 1997 that it would not produce or employ chemical weapons, including biological toxins. However, the CIA reported in June 1997 that Iran had obtained new dual-use technology from China and India during 1996.

The CIA reported in January 1999 that Iran continued to pursue dual-use biotechnical equipment from Russia and other countries, ostensibly for civilian uses. Its biological warfare (BW) program began during the Iran-Iraq War, and Iran may have some limited capability for BW deployment. Outside assistance is both important and difficult to prevent, given the dual-use nature of the materials and equipment being sought and the many legitimate end uses for these items.

In 2001, an allegation surfaced from the former director of research and development at the Cuban Center for Genetic Engineering and Biotechnology claiming that Cuba had assisted the Iranian bioweapons program from 1995 to 1998. The authenticity of the director's claims has not been established.[4]

A report produced by the Iranian insurgent group, the Mojahedin Khalq Organization, asserted in 2003 that Iran had started producing weaponized anthrax and was actively working with at least five other pathogens, including smallpox. The Mojahedin Khalq Organization was the same organization that had produced early evidence of Iran's noncompliance with the terms of the Nuclear Non-Proliferation Treaty (NPT). Iran issued a vehement denial of these charges in a May 16, 2003, press release. The accuracy of either set of statements is uncertain.

The CIA reported in November 2003 that "even though Iran is part of the Biological Weapons Convention (BWC), Tehran probably maintained an offensive BW program. Iran continued to seek dual-use biotechnical materials, equipment, and expertise. Though such materials had legitimate uses, Iran's BW program also could have benefited from them. It is likely that Iran has capabilities to produce small quantities of BW agents but has a limited ability to weaponize them."

Russia remains a key source of biotechnology for Iran. Russia's world-leading expertise in biological weapons makes it an attractive target for Iranians seeking technical information and training on BW agent production processes. Iran may have the production technology to make dry storable and aerosol weapons. This would allow it to develop suitable missile warheads, bombs, and covert devices.

THE STATUS OF THE IRANIAN NUCLEAR PROGRAM

As was noted above, Iran has denied that it is developing nuclear weapons since such reports first surfaced in the early 1970s, at the time of the shah. Since that time, evidence has surfaced again and again that Iran may be lying and that many of its "peaceful" nuclear activities are actually under the direct or indirect control of the IRGC. However, there has never been conclusive evidence that Iran was developing a weapon.

There are also long periods since the fall of the shah for which very few data are available on any aspect of Iran's nuclear efforts, leaving serious gaps in the historical flow of the evidence. Iran has also always claimed to comply with arms control agreements, and it has always found an explanation for each new discovery that claims its actions were peaceful and either research programs or efforts to create a national nuclear power program.

The end result is a long list of nuclear programs and facilities that are at best ambiguous in character. Taken as a body of evidence, they provide strong indications that Iran began a nuclear weapons program under the shah, and that the Ayatollah Rhuholla Khomeini revived this program after Iraq began to use chemical weapons against Iran during the Iran-Iraq War. Though Iran has continued to state that it is not developing nuclear weapons, and some of its clerics have said such weapons are against Islamic principles, senior Iranian officials and clerics have also asserted Iran's right to have nuclear weapons and the kind of nuclear fuel cycle that Iran could use to produce weapons grade materials.

THE UNCERTAIN CHARACTER OF IRAN'S NUCLEAR FACILITIES

Iran has a long list of known and suspect nuclear facilities, many of which have raised serious questions regarding their character and Iran's nuclear research, development, and production facilities. Iran also has a large and well-dispersed mix of state industries and military facilities that it can use to hide its activities or to shelter and disperse them.

There are no accurate unclassified lists of such Iranian facilities, and claims have been made in various press and opposition sources over the years that Iran is carrying out parts of a nuclear weapons program in a wide range of sites—only some of which have turned out to be real or probable. Work by GlobalSecurity.org has examined these various reports and claims in depth.[5] The following list and subsequent discussion of each facility are drawn from this work and are combined with recent reporting by the IAEA on what is and is not known about the nature of Iran's activities in each facility.[6] This material shows how difficult it is to understand the overall structure of Iran's activities and the scale of Iran's activities, to know whether or not they are weapons related, and to know enough to target them. The facilities are:

- Anarak waste storage site
- Arak
- Ardekan (Ardakan) nuclear fuel site
- Bushehr: nuclear facility and light water nuclear power reactor
- Chalus

- Covert reactor?

- Darkhovin

- Esfahan (Isfahan) Nuclear Technology/Research Center

- Gchine uranium mine

- Karaj / Karai / Hashtgerd Nuclear Research Center for Agriculture and Medicine

- Kolahdouz (Kolahdouz, Kolahdooz, or Kolahdoz) nuclear facility

- Lashkar Ab'ad pilot plant for isotope separation

- Lavizan I and II Nuclear Weapons Development Center

- Meysami Research Center

- Natanz (Kashan) facility

- Parchin

- Qatran Workshop in Central Iran

- Saghand (Sagend) uranium ore deposit in Yazd

- Tabas?

- Tehran / Tehran Vicinity Tehran Nuclear Research Center and Kalaye Electric Company

- Uranium Mines and Facilities

Anarak Waste Storage Site. Iran has stated that small amounts of imported UO_2 were prepared for targets at the Jabr Ibn Hayan Multipurpose Laboratories (JHL), irradiated at the Tehran Research Reactor (TRR), and sent to a laboratory belonging to the MIX Facility in Tehran for separation of I-131 in a lead-shielded cell. Iran has informed the IAEA that the remaining nuclear waste was solidified and eventually transferred to a waste disposal site at Anarak. There reportedly is uranium ore near Anarak, not far from Yazd. The Talmessi Mine (Talmesi Mine), near Anarak, has produced Seelite with occurs with Uranospinite.

Arak. The IAEA reports that "... Iran is in the process of constructing the IR-40 reactor at Arak (although originally planned to be built at Esfahan, a decision is said to have been taken in 2002 to build the reactor at Arak instead). The basic design of the IR-40 was completed in 2002, and provides for the use of natural uranium oxide as fuel. It is planned to go into operation in 2014. ... The IR-40 is said to have been based on indigenous design. The purpose of the reactor was declared to be research and development and the production of radioisotopes for medical and industrial use.

"Iran is also building a heavy water production plant (HWPP) at Arak, and has said that it intends to start producing heavy water there in 2004.... In its letter of 21 October 2003, Iran acknowledged that two hot cells had been foreseen for the reactor project. In that letter, Iran also made reference to its plans for nine hot cells for the production of radioisotopes (molybdenum, iodine, xenon, cobalt-60 and iridium-192); specifically, 'four for the production of radioisotopes, two for the production of cobalt and iridium and three for waste management processing' (along with ten back-up manipulators). According to the information provided in that letter, however, neither the design nor detailed information about the dimensions or the actual layout of the hot cells were available yet, since the Iranian authorities did not know the characteristics of the manipulators and lead glass shielding windows which they could procure.

"In its letter of 21 October 2003, Iran acknowledged that two hot cells had been foreseen for the reactor project. In that letter, Iran also made reference to its plans for nine hot cells for the production of radioisotopes (molybdenum, iodine, xenon, cobalt-60 and iridium-192); specifically, 'four for the production of radioisotopes, two for the production of cobalt and iridium and three for waste.... In the IR-40 design information provided by Iran in November 2003, Iran confirmed that it had tentative plans for a building, in the proximity of the IR-40 facilities, with hot cells for the production of "long lived radioisotopes."' Iran agreed to submit the relevant preliminary design information with respect to that building in due course. In May 2004, Iran provided updated design information for the reactor, in which it noted that the planning of hot cells for 'long lived radioisotopes' was no longer under consideration in light of difficulties with the procurement of equipment."

Iran has informed the IAEA that it carried laboratory scale experiments to produce heavy water at the Esfahan Nuclear Technology Centre, and that two hot cells had been foreseen for its project at Arak, and that yet another building with hot cells is planned for the production of radioisotopes. Iran appears to be at least five years away from completing the heavy water reactor at Arak. According to reports published in Russia, apparently based on information developed by the

Russian Federal Security Service, facilities located at Arak are involved in the research and development (R&D) of unguided missiles, and modifications of the Scud-S missile.

Ardekan (Ardakan) Nuclear Fuel Site. This site is reportedly scheduled to be completed in mid-2005, and some reports indicate that a uranium mill with an annual capacity of 120,000 metric tons of ore and an annual output of 50 metric tons of uranium is being built 35 kilometers north of Ardakan city. The IAEA reported on November 15, 2004, that "[t]he ore is to be processed into uranium ore concentrate (UOC/yellowcake) at the associated mill at Ardakan, the Yellowcake Production Plant. The design capacity of the mill corresponds to that of the mine (50 t [tons] of uranium per year). The mill startup is forecast to coincide with the start of mining at Saghand. The mill site is currently at an early stage of development; the installation of the infrastructure and processing buildings has been started. In the south of Iran, near Bandar Abbas, Iran has constructed the Gchine uranium mine and its co-located mill. The low but variable grade uranium ore found in near-surface deposits will be open-pit mined and processed at the associated mill. The estimated production design capacity is 21 t of uranium per year. Iran has stated that, as of July 2004, mining operations had started and the mill had been hot tested, during which testing a quantity of about 40 to 50 kg of yellowcake was produced."[7]

Bushehr: Nuclear Facility and Light Water Nuclear Power Reactor. Unit 1 of this facility is a 1,000 megawatt (electric) light water reactor designed to use low enriched uranium oxide (up to 5 percent U-235). According to IAEA estimates made in November 2004, it is scheduled to reach first criticality in 2006. The reactor is being built by Russia. Some 600 to 1,000 Russians are now working on the project. Some 750 Iranian technicians, trained in Russia, will take over the plan once it becomes operational.

It will use some 90 tons of Russian supplied enriched uranium and is located at the site of a German-built reactor project that the shah commissioned in the 1970s and that was bombed during the Iran-Iraq War. The new reactor is being built to Russian designs. There are two reactor sites at Bushehr, and no work is taking place on the second site. The reactor's design is not suited to produce high levels of plutonium (Pu), as long as it operates as designed, and it would present problems because of the amount of Pu-240 produced relative to Pu-239. It can, however, be used to produce more weapons grade materials by changing the fuel loading cycle of the reactor and also to develop the skills and technology necessary to produce other reactor designs better suited to producing weapons grade plutonium.[8] Iran is considering the construction of three to five more power reactor facilities, which may or may not be located at Bushehr. Press reports indicate that several batteries of U.S.-made Hawk (Improved) Surface-to-Air Missiles have been placed around Bushehr.

Chalus. Chalus has been reported as a potential location for of an underground nuclear weapons development facility located inside a mountain south of this coastal town. The facility has been variously reported as being staffed by experts from Russia, China, and North Korea.

Covert Reactor? Unconfirmed reports have been made of a covert reactor(s) at Arak, Chalus, Darkhovin, and Tabas. Debates exist over any plans to create such reactors and whether their heat profiles could be concealed from satellite and other infrared sensors.

Darkhovin. This facility (also referred to as Ahvaz, Darkhouin, Esteghlal, and Karun) is a suspected underground nuclear weapons facility of unspecified nature reported to be under the control of the IRGC and located on the Karun River south of the city of Ahvaz.

Esfahan (Isfahan) Nuclear Technology/Research Center (ENTC). This facility is operated by the University of Esfahan, is Iran's largest nuclear research center, and is said to employ as many as 3,000 scientists. The ENTC is said to include a fuel fabrication laboratory, uranium chemistry laboratory, uranium conversion facility (UCF), and fuel manufacturing plant. Two reactors, subject to IAEA inspection, are located at the ENTC: the Miniaturized Neutron Source Reacto, a 30 kilowatt light water reactor in operation since the mid-1990s, which uses uranium/aluminum alloy (U/Al) fuel enriched to 90.2 percent U-235; and the Heavy Water Zero Power Reactor (HWZPR), also located at ENTC—a heavy water reactor, in operation since the mid-1990s, which uses natural uranium metal fuel. Iran also has a light water subcritical reactor using uranium metal fuel, which operates a few days out of the year, and a decommissioned graphite subcritical reactor that also used uranium metal fuel.

According to some sources, the ENTC is the primary location of the Iranian nuclear weapons program, with its main buildings located at

Roshandasht, 15 kilometers southeast of Esfahan. At one point, Iran sought to build a uranium hexafluoride (UF_6) conversion plant at the center with Chinese assistance. The IAEA did find that Iran performed at least some unreported plutonium separation experiments at this facility. Esfahan is the location of Iran's largest missile assembly and production plant and is reported to be the location of a chemical weapons production facility. (Other rumored locations are at Damghan, Parchin, and Qazvin.) Many conventional military facilities are in the area, including facilities for munitions productions, tank overhaul, and helicopter and fixed wing aircraft maintenance. The main operational facilities for the army's aviation units are located at Esfahan, presumably at Khatamin Air Base northeast of the city.

The IAEA has made the facility at Esfahan a key focus of its investigations. Its November 2004 report noted that "Iran carried out most of its experiments in uranium conversion between 1981 and 1993 at TNRC [Tehran Nuclear Research Center] and at the Esfahan Nuclear Technology Centre (ENTC), with some experiments (e.g., those involving pulse columns) being carried out through early 2002. In 1991, Iran entered into discussions with a foreign supplier for the construction at Esfahan of an industrial scale conversion facility. Construction on the facility, UCF, was begun in the late 1990s. UCF consists of several conversion lines, principal among which is the line for the conversion of UOC to UF_6 with an annual design production capacity of 200 tons of uranium as UF_6. The UF_6 is to be sent to the uranium enrichment facilities at Natanz, where it will be enriched up to 5 percent U-235 and the product and tails returned to UCF for conversion into low-enriched UO_2 and depleted uranium metal. The design information for UCF provided by Iran indicates that conversion lines are also foreseen for the production of natural and enriched (19.7%) uranium metal, and natural UO_2. The natural and enriched (5% U-235) UO_2 are to be sent to the Fuel Manufacturing Plant (FMP) at Esfahan, where Iran has said it will be processed into fuel for a research reactor and power reactors. In March 2004, Iran began testing the process lines involving the conversion of UOC into UO_2 and UF_4, and UF_4 into UF_6. As of June 2004, 40 to 45 kg of UF_6 had been produced therefrom. A larger test, involving the conversion of 37 t of yellowcake into UF_4, was initiated in August 2004. According to Iran's declaration of 14 October 2004, 22.5 tons of the 37 tons of yellowcake had been fed into the process and that approximately 2 tons of UF_4, and 17.5 tons of uranium as intermediate products and waste, had been produced. There was no indication as of that date of UF_6 having been produced during this later campaign. Iran has stated that UCF was to have been constructed under a turn-key contract with a foreign supplier, but that when the contract was cancelled in 1997, Iran retained the engineering designs and used them as the basis to construct UCF with Iranian resources. Iran provided preliminary design information to the Agency in July 2000. The Agency has been carrying out continuous design information verification (DIV) since that time. The Agency's enquiry into the chronology and scope of Iran's uranium conversion activities has focused on two central issues: (a) assessment of Iran's statements concerning the basis for its design of UCF (including conversion experiments), with a view to ascertaining whether Iran has declared all of its activities involving nuclear material; and (b) assessment of the declared intended uses for the products of the various UCF process lines.

". . . In 1985, Iran brought into operation a Fuel Fabrication Laboratory (FFL) at Esfahan, about which it informed the Agency in 1993 and for which design information was provided to the Agency in 1998. It is still in operation, and is suitable for producing, on a small scale, fuel pellets. The fuel manufacturing plant to be constructed at Esfahan (FMP) is scheduled to be commissioned in 2007. According to the preliminary design information that has been provided by Iran, the facility is planned to produce 40 tons per year of UO_2 fuel (with a maximum enrichment of 5%) for research and power reactors. Iran is also building a Zirconium Production Plant (ZPP) at Esfahan which, when complete, will have a capacity to produce 10 tons of zirconium tubing per year. . . . In a letter dated 5 May 2003, Iran informed the Agency of its plan to commence in 2003 the construction of FMP. On 1 November 2003, Iran submitted preliminary design information for FMP stating that the plant capacity would be 30 t UO_2 per year. On 31 August 2004, Iran submitted updated design information which reflected an increase in plant capacity to 40 t UO_2 per year, declared to have been to accommodate the fuel needs for the Bushehr Nuclear Power Plant (BNPP) (about 25 t UO_2 per year) and the 40 MW pressurized heavy water research reactor (IR-40) (about 10 t UO_2 per year)."

Gchine Uranium Mine. The IAEA reported on November 15, 2004, that "Iran has constructed the Gchine uranium mine and its co-located mill. The low but variable grade uranium ore found in near-surface deposits will be open-pit mined and processed at the associated mill. The estimated production design capacity is 21 t of uranium per year. Iran has stated that, as of July 2004, mining operations had started and the mill had been hot tested, during which testing a quantity of about 40 to 50 kg of yellowcake was produced. . . . Iran provided information to the Agency on the location, operational status and estimated annual production capacity of the Gchine mine and mill, the Saghand Mine and the Yellowcake Production Plant. The Agency carried out complementary access at Gchine on 17 July 2004, at the Saghand Mine on 6 October 2004 and at the Ardakan Yellowcake Production Plant on 7 October 2004, in the course of which the Agency was able to confirm the declared status of these operations."[9] Iran also explored potential uranium production through the production of yellowcake using percolation leaching. Iran produced an estimated several hundred kilograms of yellowcake using temporary facilities, now dismantled, located at the Gchine mining site.

Karaj / Karai / Hashtgerd Nuclear Research Center for Agriculture and Medicine. This facility, some 160 kilometers northwest of Tehran, includes a building with a dosimetry laboratory and an agricultural radiochemistry laboratory. Other buildings will house a calutron electromagnetic isotope separation system purchased from China for obtaining target materials to be radiated with neutron streams in a 30 million electron volt cyclotron. These are research systems that are not easily adaptable to nuclear weapons design efforts. There may also be a facility nearby for rocket R&D and production.

The IAEA reports that "[i]n its letter dated 21 October 2003, Iran finally acknowledged that, between 1975 and 1998, it had concluded contracts related to laser enrichment using both [atomic vapor laser isotope separation, or AVLIS] and [molecular laser isotope separation, or MLIS] techniques with four foreign entities. In the letter, Iran provided detailed information on the various contracts, and acknowledged that it had carried out laser enrichment experiments using previously undeclared imported uranium metal at TNRC between 1993 and 2000, and that it had established a pilot plant for laser enrichment at Lashkar Ab'ad, where it had also carried out experiments using imported uranium metal. According to information provided subsequently by the Iranian authorities, the equipment used there had been dismantled in May 2003, and transferred to Karaj for storage together with the uranium metal used in the experiments, before the Agency was permitted to visit Lashkar Ab'ad in August 2003. The equipment and material were presented to Agency inspectors at Karaj on 28 October 2003.

"During the Agency's complementary access to the mass spectrometry laboratories at Karaj in December 2003, the Agency examined two mass spectrometers that had not been included in Iran's declaration of 21 October 2003. Iran acknowledged that the mass spectrometers had been used at Karaj in the past to provide analytical services (isotope enrichment measurements) to the AVLIS programme, and gave the Agency a list of samples that had been analyzed. The Agency collected environmental samples from the mass spectrometers; no uranium particles were found in these samples. As requested by the Agency following complementary access at Karaj, Iran submitted additional information to the Agency on 5 January 2004 to clarify the role of the mass spectrometers in relation to Iran's uranium enrichment programme. The laboratory containing the equipment is now part of the safeguarded facility at Karaj."

Kolahdouz (Kolahdouz, Kolahdooz, or Kolahdoz) Nuclear Facility. This facility (14 kilometers west of Tehran), the location of some of Iran's armored weapons production facilities, is a large complex that the Mujahideen-e Khalq (MEK) claims has a concealed nuclear weapons plant, including uranium enrichment, and operates as a supplement to the uranium enrichment site in Natanz. A technical team of the IAEA visited the industrial complex in Kolahdouz; no work was seen at those locations that could be linked to uranium enrichment, but environmental samples were taken.

Lashkar Ab'ad Pilot Plant for Isotope Separation. The IAEA reports that "Iran established a pilot plant at Lashkar Ab'ad in 2002, where it conducted laser enrichment experiments in December 2002 and January 2003. Iran dismantled the equipment in May 2003. Iran has stated that it currently has no plans to resume the enrichment of uranium using laser isotope separation (LIS). It has indicated that it is continuing with its R&D on laser activities, such as those involving copper vapor lasers (CVLs) and Nd:YAG lasers, but that that work is not part of a programme to use such lasers for uranium enrichment.

". . . While the contract for the AVLIS facility at Lashkar Ab'ad was specifically written for the delivery of a system that could demonstrably achieve enrichment levels of 3.5% to 7%, it is the opinion of Agency experts that the system, as designed and reflected in the contract, would have been capable of HEU [highly enriched uranium] production had the entire package of equipment been delivered. In response to Agency questions in connection with this assessment, Iran referred to the contract and the design parameters contained therein, and provided information demonstrating the very limited capabilities of the equipment actually delivered to Iran under this contract to produce HEU (i.e., only in gram quantities). Iranian AVLIS researchers maintain that they were not aware of the significance of these features when they negotiated and contracted for the supply and delivery of the Lashkar Ab'ad AVLIS facility.

". . . The Agency has completed its review of Iran's AVLIS programme and has concluded that Iran's descriptions of the levels of enrichment achieved using AVLIS at the TNRC CSL [Comprehensive Separation Laboratory] and at Lashkar Ab'ad and the amounts of material used in its past activities are consistent with information available to the Agency to date. Iran has presented all declared key equipment, which has been verified by the Agency. If, as stated by Iran, the evaporated uranium and some collectors were discarded as waste, mainly at the Qom disposal site, recovery of the small quantities of nuclear material involved would not be feasible and therefore accurate nuclear material accountancy is not possible. The Agency will continue to monitor laser related activities in Iran as a routine safeguards implementation matter."

Lavizan I and II Nuclear Weapons Development Center. Some analysts claimed in December 2004 that Iran was testing conventional explosives at this site (in northeastern Tehran) in ways indicating that they might be used to simulate nuclear explosions and test high-explosive lenses and warheads. The IAEA has satellite photos that seem to support this possibility but cannot inspect without Iran's permission because this is not a declared facility.[10]

Meysami Research Center. This facility is located at kilometer 27 of the Karaj Special Road. Its principal activity is as chemical agent detector, and it may have a role in chemical and nuclear weapons efforts.

Natanz [Kashan] Facility. This facility is located between Esfahan and Kashan in central Iran, about 100 miles north of Esfahan, in old Kashan-Natanz. It is reported to be a covert facility for heavy water production and centrifuge enrichment activity. The IAEA had found particles of highly enriched uranium in environmental samples taken at Natanz in August 2003. The machines the IAEA found at the Pilot Fuel Enrichment Plant (PFEP) were early European designs of Pakistani origin. Iran stated that it did not carry out enrichment and that no nuclear material was introduced to the PFEP prior to IAEA sampling. The IAEA sampling found two types of highly enriched uranium and some 1,000 centrifuges under construction.

There is a fuel enrichment plant (FEP) of some 100,000 square meters, which the MEK claims has two 25,000-meter halls, built 8 meters deep into the ground and protected by a concrete wall 2.5 meters thick, According to some estimates, it could house as many as 50,000 centrifuges, producing enough weapons grade uranium for 20 weapons per year. Other estimates suggest a total of 5,000 centrifuges capable of producing enough enriched uranium for several nuclear weapons a year. By mid-2004 the Natanz centrifuge facility was hardened with a roof of several meters of reinforced concrete and buried under a layer of earth some 23 meters deep.

The MEK claims that parts for centrifuges were imported and that others were built at a plant in Esfahan. They were then tested at the Kalaye plant in Ab-Ali and sent to Natanz for final assembly. Two villages near Natanz—called Lashgarabad and Ramandeh—have uranium enrichment plants hidden behind trees in orchards and were surrounded by security guards and function as a backup to the Natanz site in case that facility came under military attack. The laboratories are reported to be in the Hasthgerd region near Karaj, about 40 kilometers (25 miles) west of Tehran. There are also reports of LIS experiments at Nantaz, as well as at Ramandeh (part of the Karaj Agricultural and Medical Centre) and a laser laboratory at Lashkar Ab'ad.

The IAEA describes a far more modest effort. It reports that "[i]n 2001, Iran began the construction of two facilities at Natanz: the smaller scale PFEP, planned to have some 1000 centrifuges for enrichment up to 5% U-235; and the large scale commercial FEP, which is planned to contain over 50 000 P-1 centrifuges for enrichment up to 5% U-235. On 25 June 2003, Iran introduced UF_6 into the first centrifuge at PFEP. As of October 2003, the installation of a 164-machine cascade was being finalized. In November 2003, the cascade was shut down. As of the Agency's latest inspection on 11 October 2004, the cascade had not been operated and no further UF_6 gas had been fed into centrifuges at PFEP. FEP has been scheduled to start receiving centrifuges in early 2005, after the design is confirmed by the tests to be conducted in PFEP. According to Iran, the only work that has been done on the P-2 design was carried out between 2002 and 2003, largely at the workshop of a private company under contract with the AEOI [Atomic Energy Organization of Iran], and the work was limited to the manufacture and mechanical testing of a small number of modified P-2 composite rotors. Iran has stated that 'no other institution (including universities), company or organization in Iran has been involved in P-2 R&D' and that 'no P-2 R&D has been undertaken by or at the request of the Ministry of Defence.' Iran has also said that all R&D on P-2 centrifuges had been terminated and that no other work on that, or any other centrifuge design, was done prior to 2002 or has been done since 2003. However, in its Additional Protocol declarations, Iran has foreseen P-2 R&D activities for the future."[11]

Parchin. Some analysts claimed in December 2004 that Iran was testing conventional explosives at this site (southeast of Tehran) in ways that indicated they might be to simulate nuclear explosions and test high-explosive lenses and warheads. The IAEA has satellite photos that seem to support this possibility but cannot inspect without Iran's permission because this is not a declared facility.[12]

Qatran Workshop in Central Iran. MEK sources have claimed that a secret nuclear facility exists at the Qatran Workshop in Central Iran, some 150 miles south of Tehran. A plant has been under construction that appears to be designed to produce heavy water. Heavy water is used to moderate the nuclear chain reaction in one type of nuclear reactor, but the nuclear reactor at Bushehr does not use heavy water. U.S. State Department spokesman Richard Boucher stated in a December 13, 2002, briefing that there was "hard evidence," that Iran appeared to be constructing a uranium enrichment plant at Nantaz, as well as a heavy water plant. "The suspect uranium-enrichment plant . . . could be used to produce highly-enriched uranium for weapons. The heavy-water plant could support a reactor for producing weapons-grade plutonium. These facilities are not justified by the needs of Iran's civilian nuclear program." Iran rejected the allegations and reiterated that the two plants were intended to generate electricity, but Iran has no known heavy water reactor and no need for an indigenous source of heavy water. Heavy-water-moderated reactors are better suited for plutonium production than are light water reactors.

Saghand (Sagend) Uranium Ore Deposit in Yazd. This facility is said to be an area of 100 to 150 square kilometers, with reserves estimated at 3,000 to 5,000 tons of uranium oxide. Some reports indicate a reserve of at least 1.58 million metric tons of uranium ore with an average grade of 533 parts per million (0.0533 percent uranium). This translates into a total uranium contents of 842 metric tons. The IAEA reported in November 2004 that "Iran has a long-standing programme of exploration for uranium deposits, and has selected two locations for development as mines. At the Saghand Mine, located in Yazd in central Iran, low-grade hard rock ore bodies will be exploited through conventional underground mining techniques. The annual estimated production design capacity is forecast as 50 t of uranium. The infrastructure and shaft sinking are essentially complete, and tunnelling towards the ore bodies has started. Ore production is forecast to start by the end of 2006. The ore is to be processed into uranium ore concentrate (UOC/yellowcake) at the associated mill at Ardakan, the Yellowcake Production Plant. The design capacity of the mill corresponds to that of the mine (50 t of uranium per year). The mill startup is forecast to coincide with the start of mining at Saghand. The mill site is currently at an early stage of development; the installation of the infrastructure and processing buildings has been started. In the south of Iran, near Bandar Abbas."[13]

Tabas? Tabas is suspected of being a site/facility, but this has not been confirmed.

Tehran / Tehran Vicinity Tehran Nuclear Research Center and Kalaye Electric Company. The research program of the Tehran-based Center for Theoretical Physics and Mathematics of the AEOI includes theoretical physics, and other R&D related to high-energy physics, including particle physics, mathematical physics, astrophysics, theoretical nuclear physics, statistical mechanics, theoretical plasma physics, and mathematics. There is a research reactor, the TRR, located at the TNRC—a 5 megawatt pool-type light water research reactor that has been in operation since the late 1960s; it originally used HEU U/Al alloy fuel, but it was reconfigured in the early 1990s and now uses fuel of U_3O_8/Al enriched to about 20 percent U-235.

The IAEA notes that "Iran has explored two other potential uranium production routes. One was the extraction of uranium from phosphoric acid. Using research scale equipment, small quantities of yellowcake were successfully produced at the . . . TNRC laboratories. Iran has stated that there are no facilities in Iran for separating uranium from phosphoric acid other than the research facilities at TNRC. . . . Iran carried out most of its experiments in uranium conversion between 1981 and 1993 at TNRC and at the . . . ENTC, with some experiments (e.g., those involving pulse columns) being carried out through early 2002. . . . In February 2003, Iran acknowledged that it had imported in 1991 natural uranium, in a variety of forms, which it had not previously reported to the Agency, and that it had used some of these materials, at locations which had not previously been reported to the Agency, for testing certain parts of the UCF conversion process (i.e., uranium dissolution, purification using pulse columns and the production of uranium metal). On a number of occasions between February and July 2003, Iran stated that this information, along with documentation provided by the foreign supplier, had been sufficient to permit Iran to complete indigenously the detailed design and manufacturing of the equipment for UCF. Iran repeatedly stated that it had not carried out any research and development (R&D) or testing, even on a laboratory scale, of other more complex processes (e.g., conversion of UO_2 to UF_4 and conversion of UF_4 to UF_6) using nuclear material.[14]

". . . Following the discovery by the Agency of indications of depleted UF_4 in samples of waste taken at the Jabr Ibn Hayan Multipurpose Laboratories (JHL) at TNRC, Iran acknowledged, in a letter dated 19 August 2003, that it had carried out UF_4 conversion experiments on a laboratory scale during the 1990s at the Radiochemistry Laboratories of TNRC using depleted uranium which had been imported in 1977 and exempted from safeguards upon receipt, and which Iran had declared in 1998 (when the material was de-exempted) as having been lost during processing. In October 2003, Iran further acknowledged that, contrary to its previous statements, practically all of the materials important to uranium conversion had been produced in laboratory and bench scale experiments (in kilogram quantities) carried out at TNRC and at ENTC between 1981 and 1993 without having been reported to the Agency. The information provided in Iran's letter of 21 October 2003 stated that, in conducting these experiments, Iran had also used yellowcake imported by Iran in 1982 but only confirmed in 1990. . . .

"In its letter of 21 October 2003, Iran acknowledged that the uranium metal had been intended not only for the production of shielding material, as previously stated, but also for use in its laser enrichment programme (the existence of which, as discussed below, Iran had previously not acknowledged, and which was only declared to the Agency in that same letter of 21 October 2003). Iran stated that the uranium metal process line at UCF had been developed by Iranian scientists at the TNRC laboratories, and that a small quantity of the metal produced at TNRC during the development tests (about 2 kg) had been given to the laser group for its evaluation.

". . . In 1985, Iran initiated its efforts in gas centrifuge enrichment with a search of available technical literature. In 1987, Iran acquired through a clandestine supply network drawings for a P-1 centrifuge, along with samples of centrifuge components. According to Iran, gas centrifuge R&D testing began at TNRC in 1988 and continued there until 1995, when those activities were moved to a workshop of the Kalaye Electric Company, a company in Tehran belonging to the . . . AEOI. Between 1994 and 1996, Iran received another—apparently duplicate—set of drawings for the P-1 centrifuge design, along with components for 500 centrifuges. According to Iran, it was at this time as well when Iran received design drawings for a P-2 centrifuge through the same network. Between 1997 and 2002, Iran assembled and tested P-1 centrifuges at the Kalaye Electric Company workshop where Iran says it fed UF_6 gas into a centrifuge for the first time in 1999 and, in 2002, fed nuclear material into a number of centrifuges (up to 19 machines).

". . . Given the inherent difficulties with investigating activities that ended over a decade ago, it is not possible to verify in detail the chronologies and descriptions of the experiments that took place in Iran.

Thus, the Agency's activities have had to focus on assessing the consistency of the information provided by Iran and examining the remaining equipment and nuclear material.

". . . Iran also acknowledged that the Kalaye Electric Company workshop in Tehran had been used for the production of centrifuge components, but stated that there had been no testing of centrifuges assembled from these components involving the use of nuclear material, either at that workshop or at any other location in Iran. . . . According to information provided at that time by Iran, the design, research and development work, which it said had been started only five years earlier (i.e., 1997), had been based on information available from open sources and extensive computer modeling and simulation, including tests of centrifuge rotors without nuclear material.

". . . In June 2003, Iran reiterated that its centrifuge R&D had commenced only in 1997, with centrifuge testing having taken place in the Plasma Physics buildings of TNRC. The Agency was shown the areas within the buildings where the testing was said to be been conducted, and was again told that no nuclear material had been used during the test programme. Based on their own observations and their discussions with Iranian authorities, the Agency enrichment technology experts concluded that it was not possible for Iran to have developed enrichment technology to the level seen at Natanz based solely on open source information, computer simulation and mechanical testing. . . . In August 2003, Iran amended these statements, informing the Agency that the decision to launch a centrifuge enrichment programme had actually been taken in 1985, and that Iran had in fact received drawings of the P-1 centrifuge through a foreign intermediary around 1987. Iran stated that the centrifuge R&D programme had been situated at TNRC between 1988 and 1995, and had been moved to the Kalaye Electric Company workshop in 1995. According to Iran, the centrifuge R&D activities were carried out at the Kalaye Electric Company workshop between 1995 and 2003, and were moved to Natanz in 2003.

"During its August 2003 visit to Iran, the Agency was shown electronic copies of the centrifuge engineering drawings (including the general arrangement, sub-assembly and component drawings). Agency inspectors were also able to visit and take environmental samples at the Kalaye Electric Company workshop, where they noted that, since their first visit to the workshop in March 2003, considerable renovation had been made to one of the buildings on the site. As was anticipated by the Agency at the time, the renovation, which was carried out in connection with Iran's attempt to conceal the activities carried out there, has interfered with the Agency's ability to resolve issues associated with Iran's centrifuge enrichment programme, since the Agency was unable to see the equipment in situ and could not take environmental samples while the equipment was there.

"In its letter of 21 October 2003, Iran finally acknowledged that 'a limited number of tests, using small amounts of UF_6,' had been conducted in 1999 and 2002 at the Kalaye Electric Company workshop. . . . In October/November 2003 and again in October 2004, Agency inspectors interviewed a former official of the AEOI, said by Iran to have been involved in its centrifuge R&D work from 1987 until he left the Kalaye Electric Company in 2001. During the latter meeting, he provided, in particular, details on the negotiations which had resulted in Iran's procurement around 1987 of the P-1 design (and sample components), and on the supply of the duplicate set of P-1 designs and the components for 500 P-1 centrifuges, delivered through intermediaries to Iran in two shipments said to have taken place in March 1994 and July 1996, and the supply of bellows in 1997 to replace previously provided poor quality bellows. He also confirmed that meetings with the intermediary continued after 1996, and included discussions on technical issues. According to the information provided by Iran, 13 official meetings took place with the clandestine supply network between 1994 and 1999. Iran has been requested to provide information on what, if any, meetings related to Iran's centrifuge programme took place prior to 1994. The Agency has also requested Iran to present the shipping documents associated with the 1994 and 1996 deliveries, and to provide information on the content of the technical discussions held with the intermediaries and explain why no meetings involving AEOI officials took place after June 1999.

"In January 2004, in response to a follow-up inquiry by the Agency on Iran's centrifuge enrichment programme, Iran acknowledged, for the first time, that it had received in 1994 P-2 centrifuge drawings from foreign sources. Iran also stated that the AEOI had concluded a contract with the owner of a private company located in Tehran to develop a P-2 centrifuge, and that some mechanical tests had been

conducted, without nuclear material, on a small number of domestically manufactured rotors based on a modified P-2 design. In its communication of 5 March 2004, Iran indicated that R&D activities on P-2
centrifuges had not been mentioned in its 21 October 2003 declaration
because 'Iran intended to submit information on P_{II} along with further
declarations it is required to provide in accordance with its obligations
under the Additional Protocol within the timetable established by the
IAEA.'

"In clarifications provided in April and May 2004, Iran stated that
the P-2 drawings had been received around 1995, but that, due to a
shortage in professional resources and changes in AEOI management,
priority was placed at that time on resolving difficulties being encoun-
tered by Iran in connection with the P-1 centrifuge, and that no actual
work on the P-2 centrifuge had commenced until after the contract
was concluded in early 2002. . . . The Agency has been able to interview
the owner of the private company on a number of occasions since
then. According to the contractor, he first saw the design for the P-2
centrifuge in early 2002, and after having received copies and review-
ing them, he had decided that, since in his view Iran was not capable of
manufacturing maraging steel cylinders with bellows, work should
proceed with a shorter, sub-critical carbon composite rotor. He explained further that he had manufactured seven rotors and had performed some mechanical tests on them, but without using nuclear
material. He said that the contract was terminated in March 2003, but
that he continued to work on his own until June 2003, and that all of
the centrifuge equipment had been moved to Pars Trash. In October
2004, the Agency also interviewed the former AEOI official referred to
above, who was said to have originally received the P-2 centrifuge design. During these discussions, he described the negotiations that had
led to the supply of the P-2 design drawings, which he recalled as having taken place around 1995 or 1996, as well as the reasons for the apparent gap of seven years before the R&D test work on the P-2 design
had begun.

". . . The Iranian authorities have stated that Iran did not obtain
any P-2 centrifuges from abroad, and that the components that it did
have had been produced domestically in the contractor's workshop,
with the exception of some raw materials and minor items supplied to
the contractor by the P-1 R&D team, and a few items which had been

purchased from abroad in connection with the P-2 contract, such as bearings, oils and magnets. The contractor acknowledged that he had made enquiries with a European intermediary about the procurement of 4000 magnets with specifications suitable for use in P-2 centrifuges and that he had also mentioned to the intermediary the possibility of much higher numbers in order to attract the supplier and to get a good price by suggesting that larger orders would follow. The Iranian authorities have stated that no magnets were actually delivered by that intermediary to Iran, but that imported magnets relevant to P-2 centrifuges had been procured from other foreign suppliers in 2002.

". . . The Agency has reiterated its previous requests for further information from Iran, along with supporting documentation, on the procurement of magnets for the P-2 centrifuges (in particular, on the sources of all such magnets), including attempted procurement and enquiries about procurement, and the procurement of any other relevant components, with a view to facilitating completion by the Agency of its assessment of the P-2 experiments said to have been carried out by the private contractor. In October 2004, Iran provided the Agency with more information in this regard, which is currently being assessed. However, there remains further information requested by the Agency that has yet to be provided. After a number of requests by the Agency, on 19 October 2004, Iran finally provided the Agency with copies of the contract and the report, which had been informally translated by Iran in April 2004. These documents appear to confirm the Iranian statements about the nature of the work requested of and carried out by the contractor between 2002 and 2003. Iran has reiterated that no work was carried out on the P-2 design (or any centrifuge design other than the P-1 design) prior to 2002. The reasons given by Iran for the apparent gap between 1995 and 2002, however, do not provide sufficient assurance that there were no related activities carried out during that period, particularly given that the contractor was able to make the modifications necessary for the composite cylinders within a short period after early 2002 when, according to Iran, he had seen the drawings for the first time. The Agency is attempting to verify this information, inter alia, through the network of suppliers.

". . . Between 1975 and 1998, Iran concluded with four foreign supplier's contracts related to laser enrichment using both . . . AVLIS and

. . . MLIS techniques. In connection with the first two contracts, the Agency has confirmed that the AVLIS spectroscopy equipment Iran received never properly functioned, and that Iran did not receive all of the components of the MLIS equipment. . . . In connection with the third contract, Iran carried out testing in the supplied Laser Separation Laboratory (LSL) and Comprehensive Separation Laboratory (CSL) at TNRC between 1993 and 2000, and dismantled the supplied equipment between 2000 and 2003.

". . . Between 1988 and 1993, Iran carried out plutonium separation experiments at TNRC. The shielded glove boxes in which these experiments were carried out were dismantled in 1993, relocated to JHL and used for other purposes. In 1995, Iran started constructing the MIX Facility. However, as the neutron flux of TRR is not sufficient for the production of the radioisotopes referred to above using natural uranium targets, the facility has not yet been commissioned. In its letter of 21 October 2003, Iran acknowledged the irradiation of depleted UO_2 targets at TRR and subsequent plutonium separation experiments in shielded glove boxes in the Nuclear Safety Building of TNRC. Neither the activities nor the separated plutonium had been reported previously to the Agency.

". . . In meetings held in Iran between 27 October and 1 November 2003, Iran provided additional information about these experiments. According to Iranian officials, the experiments took place between 1988 and 1993, and involved pressed or sintered UO_2 pellets prepared at ENTC using depleted uranium that had been exempted from safeguards in 1978. Iran stated that the capsules containing the pellets had been irradiated in TRR in connection with a project to produce fission product isotopes of molybdenum, iodine and xenon, and that some of the capsules had been processed and the plutonium separated. The plutonium separation was carried out at TNRC in three shielded glove boxes, which, according to Iran, were dismantled in 1993 and moved to the JHL building, where the glove boxes were used for iodine production until 1999. They were dismantled in 1999, decontaminated and sent to ENTC in 2000, where they have been stored along with related equipment since then. Iran has stated that these experiments were carried out to learn about the nuclear fuel cycle, and to gain experience in reprocessing chemistry.

"... On 8 November 2003, the Agency was able to take samples from the separated plutonium, which was presented to the Agency in the form of plutonium solution contained in two bottles, one of which had completely leaked out of its container. During their inspection at JHL, Agency inspectors were also shown four heavily shielded containers said by Iran to contain the unprocessed irradiated targets. The containers had been buried on the site of TNRC, but were dug up and presented to the Agency for verification. Using available non-destructive analysis equipment, Agency inspectors were able to confirm that one of the containers (selected at random) contained highly radioactive material characteristic of irradiated targets. All four containers have been placed under Agency seal for future examination.

"... [O]n the basis of information available to it as of November 2003, the Agency concluded: that the amount of separated plutonium declared by Iran had been understated (quantities in the milligram range rather than the microgram range as stated by Iran); that the plutonium samples taken from a glove box said to have been involved had plutonium-240 (Pu-240) abundance higher than that found in the plutonium solution bottles presented; that there was an excess amount of americium-241 (Am-241) in the samples; and that the age of the plutonium solution in the bottles appeared to be less than the declared 12–16 years. . . . On the basis of a subsequent recalculation carried out by it using corrected irradiation data and a corrected equation, Iran acknowledged in May 2004 that its theoretical estimations of the quantities of plutonium produced had been understated (micrograms rather than milligrams) and accepted the Agency's estimate of about 100 mg as having been correct.

"... [I]n early August 2004, the Agency explained in detail the methodology it had used for dating the plutonium that had been separated, and additional on going work to validate the results. The Iranian officials reiterated their previous statement that the experiments had been completed in 1993 and that no plutonium had been separated since then. The Agency agreed to further analyze the available data. On 15 September 2004, a new set of samples was taken from the plutonium solution. The preliminary results of the analyses of the samples thus far are the same as those previously obtained, indicating that the plutonium could have been separated after 1993. On

29 October 2004, the Agency requested additional clarifications, which are needed for a final assessment.

". . . Between 1989 and 1993, Iran irradiated two bismuth targets, and attempted to extract polonium from one of them, at TRR as part of a feasibility study for the production of neutron sources. Iran has stated that it does not have a project either for the production of Po-210 or for the production of neutron sources using Po-210 and that 'there [had] not been in the past any studies or projects on the production of neutron sources using Po-210.' . . . In September 2003, the Agency noticed from TRR operating records that bismuth metal samples had been irradiated during the same general period as the reprocessing experiments had been carried out (1989–1993). Although bismuth is not nuclear material requiring declaration under a comprehensive safeguards agreement, the irradiation of bismuth is of interest to the Agency as it produces polonium-210 (Po-210), an intensely radioactive alpha emitting radioisotope that can be used not only for certain civilian applications (such as radioisotope thermoelectric generators, or RTGs; in effect, nuclear batteries), but also, in conjunction with beryllium, for military purposes (specifically, as a neutron initiator in some designs of nuclear weapons).

". . . In the meeting on 21 May 2004, Iranian authorities continued to maintain that the purpose of the bismuth irradiation had been to produce pure Po-210 on a laboratory scale, noting that, if production and extraction of Po-210 were successful, it could be used in radioisotope thermoelectric batteries, as was the case in the SNAP-3 application (a U.S.-developed power source for use in space probes). . . . The Agency has requested access to the glove box used for the Po-210 separation; however, according to Iran, the glove box has been discarded. The Agency has also requested to see the original project proposal by the scientists involved seeking permission to carry out the project. Iran has stated that the original documentation could not be found, and has provided instead a document that it has certified as being a 'correct accurate and authentic' copy."

Uranium Mines/Facilities. Since 1988, Iran has reportedly opened as many as 10 uranium mines, including the Saghand uranium mine in Yazd province, as well otherwise unspecified locations in Khorassan, Sistan va Baluchestan, and Hormozgan provinces, and in Bandar-e-Abbas and Badar-e-Lengeh provinces along the Gulf. Iran, however, is not rich in uranium resources, and it only has proven reserves of about 3,000 tons, although its resources could be as high as 20,000 to 30,000 tons of U-308.

NUCLEAR DEVELOPMENTS IN 2003 AND 2004

The latest round of serious charges and claims of innocence led Iran to agree with France, Germany, and the United Kingdom in October 2003 that it would (1) sign the IAEA Additional Protocol allowing improved inspection, (2) continue to cooperate with the IAEA, (3) voluntarily suspend all uranium enrichment and reprocessing activities as defined by the IAEA, and (4) engage in full cooperation with the IAEA to address and resolve all outstanding issues.[15]

Iran did sign the protocols on December 18, 2003, but it did not ratify them and has severely restricted the IAEA's inspections to known and declared nuclear facilities or inspection only by prior agreement on limited terms. It also became clear during 2004 that Iran was not prepared to fully cooperate, that there were many new issues that remained unresolved, and that Iran's actions were anything but "transparent." Furthermore, on June 24, 2004, Iran declared that it would continue to manufacture centrifuges and experiment with uranium hexaflouride, two of the activities of most concern to the IAEA.[16]

Baqer Zolqadr, the commander of the IRGC, also stated in August 2004 that any Israeli attack on Iran would have "terrifying consequences" and that Israel would have to "permanently forget" about its nuclear research center and reactor at Dimona. He also warned that "the entire Zionist territory . . . is now within the range of Iran's advanced missiles."[17]

Reports by the director general of the IAEA—dated September 1, 2004, and October 15, 2004—provided detailed descriptions of unresolved issues, such as low and highly enriched uranium contamination in Iranian nuclear sites. They also provided significant indications that Iran continues its nuclear development program. They indicated it has already sought to create centrifuge enrichment facilities, has experimented with LIS, and may have a design for more advanced P-2 centrifuges. They did not confirm that Iran was actively pursuing nuclear weapons, and Iran once again cited a number of other explanations for its activities. They did, however, cite case after case where major questions remain and that suggest that Iran does seem committed to a nuclear weapons program.

Evidence also surfaced that Pakistan may have helped Iran in its enrichment program. The IAEA reports indicated that Pakistan has helped Iran since 1995, and may have delivered the P-2 design to the Iranians. The IAEA warned that Iran intended to "turn 37 tons of nearly raw uranium called yellowcake, into uranium hexafluoride." Experts contend that this could be enough to create five to six atomic weapons.[18]

The future nature of Iran's efforts is uncertain, but the process of discovery, Iranian counterclaims, and new negotiations seems unchanging. On November 15, 2004, Iran and the European Union reached an agreement that read in part:

> To build further confidence, Iran has decided, on a voluntary basis, to continue and extend its suspension to include all enrichment related and reprocessing activities, and specifically: the manufacture and import of gas centrifuges and their components; the assembly, installation, testing or operation of gas centrifuges; work to undertake any plutonium separation, or to construct or operate any plutonium separation installation; and all tests or production at any uranium conversion installation. The IAEA will be notified of this suspension and invited to verify and monitor it. The suspension will be implemented in time for the IAEA to confirm before the November Board that it has been put into effect. The suspension will be sustained while negotiations proceed on a mutually acceptable agreement on long-term arrangements.[19]

Iran also agreed to declare that it did not and would not seek to acquire nuclear weapons; that it would honor the Additional Protocol, pending its ratification; that it would comprehensively halt all enrichment and reprocessing activities, including centrifuges and plutonium separation; and that it would develop longer-term cooperation agreements with the IAEA to ensure that its nuclear activities were peaceful in return for trade incentives and the transfer of nuclear technology from Europe.[20]

This change in the Iranian position seems to have been motivated by fear of sanctions imposed by the UN Security Council, and it triggered Iran's agreement to suspend its nuclear program three days before the IAEA met in Vienna on November 25, 2004. On November 22, the Iranians announced that "to build confidence and in line with implementing the Paris Agreement, Iran suspended uranium enrichment (and related activities) as of today." The Associated Press quoted the Iranian Foreign Ministry's spokesman, Hamid Reza Asefi, as saying that "Iran's acceptance of suspension is a political decision, not an obligation, [which is] the best decision under the current circumstances.[21]

The head of the IAEA, Mohamed El Baradei, said at the time of the agreement that he thought "everything has come to a halt."[22] However, the report the IAEA had issued a few weeks earlier did not exonerate Iran of its nuclear ambitions. In fact, the report pointed out that "[b]ased on all the information currently available to the Agency, it is clear that Iran has failed in a number of instances over an extended period of time to meet its obligations under its Safeguards Agreement with respect to the reporting of nuclear material, its processing and its use, as well as the declaration of facilities where such material has been stored." The IAEA also summarized the failures of Iran as failure to report, failure to declare, failure to provide design information, and finally a failure to facilitate the implementation of the safeguards.[23]

To quote the summary in the IAEA report of October 30, 2004:

> Based on all information currently available to the Agency, it is clear that Iran has failed in a number of instances over an extended period of time to meet its obligations under its Safeguards Agreement with respect to the reporting of nuclear material, its processing and its use, as well as the declaration of facilities where such material has been processed and stored. In his June, August and November 2003 reports to the Board of Governors (GOV/2003/40, GOV/2003/63, and GOV/2003/75), the Director General identified a number of instances of such failures and the corrective actions that were being, or needed to be, taken with respect thereto by Iran.
>
> 86. As assessed in light of all information available to date, these failures can now be summarized as follows:
>
> a. Failure to report:
>
>   (i) the import of natural uranium in 1991, and its subsequent transfer for further processing;
>
>   (ii) the activities involving the subsequent processing and use of the imported natural uranium, including the production and loss of nuclear material where appropriate, and the production and transfer of waste resulting therefrom;

(iii) the use of imported natural UF6 for the testing of centrifuges at the Kalaye Electric Company workshop in 1999 and 2002, and the consequent production of enriched and depleted uranium;

(iv) the import of natural uranium metal in 1993 and its subsequent transfer for use in laser enrichment experiments, including the production of enriched uranium, the loss of nuclear material during these operations and the production and transfer of resulting waste;

(v) the production of UO2, UO3, UF4, UF6 and ammonium uranyl carbonate (AUC) from imported depleted UO2, depleted U3O8 and natural U3O8, and the production and transfer of resulting wastes; and

(vi) the production of natural and depleted UO2 targets at ENTC and their irradiation in TRR, the subsequent processing of those targets, including the separation of plutonium, the production and transfer of resulting waste, and the storage of unprocessed irradiated targets at TNRC.

b. Failure to declare:

(i) the pilot enrichment facility at the Kalaye Electric Company workshop; and

(ii) the laser enrichment plants at TNRC and the pilot uranium laser enrichment plant at Lashkar Ab'ad.

c. Failure to provide design information, or updated design information, for:

(i) the facilities where the natural uranium imported in 1991 (including wastes generated) was received, stored and processed (JHL, TRR, ENTC, waste storage facility at Esfahan and Anarak);

(ii) the facilities at ENTC and TNRC where UO2, UO3, UF4, UF6 and AUC from imported depleted UO2, depleted U3O8 and natural U3O8 were produced;

(iii) the waste storage at Esfahan and at Anarak, in a timely manner;

(iv) the pilot enrichment facility at the Kalaye Electric Company workshop;

(v) the laser enrichment plants at TNRC and Lashkar Ab'ad, and locations where resulting wastes were processed and stored, including the waste storage facility at Karaj; and

(vi) TRR, with respect to the irradiation of uranium targets, and the facility at TNRC where plutonium separation took place, as well as the waste handling facility at TNRC.

d. Failure on many occasions to cooperate to facilitate the implementation of safeguards, as evidenced by extensive concealment activities.

87. As corrective actions, Iran has submitted inventory change reports (ICRs) relevant to all of these activities, provided design information with respect to the facilities where those activities took place, and presented all declared nuclear material for Agency verification, and it

undertook in October 2003 to implement a policy of cooperation and full transparency.

On November 17, 2004, the U.S. secretary of state, Colin Powell, reiterated that Iran has not given up its determination to acquire a nuclear weapon or a delivery system that is capable of carrying such weapon. "I have seen some information that would suggest that they have been actively working on delivery systems. . . . You don't have a weapon until you put it in something that can deliver a weapon. . . . I am not talking about uranium or fissile material or the warhead; I'm talking about what one does with a warhead," Secretary Powell announced.[24]

In early December 2004, several U.S. intelligence experts gave a background briefing that followed upon Secretary Powell's statements. They indicated that they were convinced that Iran was aggressively seeking to develop a nuclear warhead for Iran's Shahab series of missile, and that Iran was actively working on the physics package for such a warhead design.[25] The U.S. officials stated that this information did not come from Iranian opposition sources like the MEK.

IRAN'S NUCLEAR WEAPONS DEVELOPMENT OPTIONS

It is far from clear whether Iran will stop its pursuit of nuclear weapons, and it may be only a matter of time before it acquires nuclear weapons. However, it is very unclear what kind of a nuclear power Iran is or will seek to be. No plans have ever surfaced as to the number and type of weapons it is seeking to produce or the nature of its delivery forces.

Iran might be content to simply develop its technology to the point where it could rapidly build a nuclear weapon. It might choose to create an undeclared deterrent and limit its weapons numbers and avoid a nuclear test. It might test and create a stockpile but not openly deploy nuclear-armed missiles or aircraft. It also, however, might create an overt nuclear force. Each option would lead to a different response for Saudi Arabia and Iran's other neighbors, as well as provoke different responses from Israel and the United States—creating different kinds of arms races, patterns of deterrence, and risks in the process.

As a result, Iran could pursue a wide range of nuclear weapons development options—many of which could be effective even if Iran was subject to many forms of preemptive attack:

- Simply carry out enough ambiguous activity to convince other nations that it has an active nuclear weapons effort, seeking to use the threat of development to create some degree of nuclear ambiguity.

- Carry out a low-level R&D effort that was covert enough to steadily move it toward a breakout capability to rapidly create weapons production capabilities but not actually build production facilities. It could maintain ambiguity by using small redundant efforts, canceling efforts when uncovered, or pausing when acute pressure came from the outside. Particularly attractive options would be developing truly advanced centrifuges or LIS facilities and completing bomb design and simulation, before beginning development of production facilities.

- Covertly develop a highly dispersed set of small and redundant production facilities, combing covert facilities like small "folded centrifuge" operations with sheltered or underground facilities. Slowly acquire actual production capability and begin stockpiling.

- Rely on covert simulation to test bomb designs and their weaponization; test a fractional weapon under the cover of an earthquake, or overtly conduct a surface test as proof of its nuclear capability.

- Appear to cancel most of its ambiguous activities, and wait until its civil nuclear reactor and technology program advances to the point where it is no longer dependent on outside supply and possibly can use some of its power reactors to obtain plutonium. Use compliance with the NPT to proliferate.

- Deploy its Shahab missiles with conventional warheads, and create a launch-on-warning or launch-under-attack capability mixed with sheltering and mobility. Arm the missiles with weapons of mass destruction once this capability is ready. Alternatively, covertly arm some missiles as soon as the Shahab and warheads are ready and/or seek at least limited missile defenses like the SA-400. Combine Shahab forces with air units and sea-based cruise missile units to create survivable and redundant forces. Either announce nuclear capability once a survivable/retaliatory force is existence or rely on nuclear ambiguity.

- Stop at fission weapons, or go on to develop "boosted" and true thermonuclear weapons.

- Stop building up a force at the level of minimal assured deterrence; participate in an open-ended arms race; seek "parity" with other regional powers like Israel—at least in terms of weapons numbers.

- Rely on an area targeting capability or develop a point target capability as well.

- Deploy satellites to improve targeting, damage assessment, and command, control, communications, computers, and intelligence (C4I) capabilities.

- Develop small weapons, and/or radiological weapons, for possible covert delivery or use by extremist and/or proxy organizations. Use the threat of transfer as a further deterrent, execute strikes in ways where deniability of responsibility has some credibility, or use actual transfer to aid in attacks or for retaliatory purposes.

It is also impossible to dismiss the possibility that Iran could respond to any decision to give up nuclear weapons by developing and producing advanced biological weapons, or that it may already have biological and nuclear efforts going on in parallel. It might also choose to develop and use "radiological weapons." Such weapons might take three forms—all of which would interact with its potential use of chemical and biological weapons:

- *The first would be a "dirty weapon"* using fissile material with contaminated or low enrichment levels that would have limited heat and blast effects but still produce yields of 3 to 5 kilotons and would effectively poison a city if detonated near the ground. Such a device would reduce some of the manufacturing and design problems inherent in creating clean or efficient nuclear weapons.

- *The second would be to use a weapon that had not been tested, that was felt to be unreliable, or that was on an inaccurate missile* and detonate it near the ground so that radiation effects would compensate for a failure to reach design efficiency or a lack of accuracy in the delivery system.

■ *The third would be to use radioactive material in micropowder or liq-*
uid form as a terror or unconventional weapon. It would be very difficult to get substantial lethality from the use of radioactive
material, and such a weapon would be less efficient than biological
weapons in weight and lethality. It would, however, have the capacity to contaminate a key area and to create a panic.

Although the United States and Russia have rejected radiological
weapons because they have the ability to precisely control the yield
from their nuclear weapons, such options might be attractive to Iran
or Iraq. As is the case with chemical and biological weapons, even the
prospect of Iran's acquiring any such nuclear weapons has increased
its ability to intimidate its neighbors.

Iran could deliver chemical, biological, or nuclear weapons on any
of its fighter-bombers, use covert delivery means, or use its missiles. It
could use its Scuds and some types of antiship missiles to deliver such
warheads relatively short distances. Its Shahab-3 missiles could probably reach virtually all the targets in Gulf countries, including many
Saudi cities on the Red Sea coast and in Western Saudi Arabia.

As discussed above, Iran's Shahab-3s are probably too inaccurate
and payload limited to be effective in delivering conventional weapons. This does not mean that conventionally armed Shahab missiles
would not use terror weapons, or weapons of intimidation, but they
could only have a major militarily impact—even against area targets—if they were armed with warheads carrying weapons of mass
destruction. Moreover, Saudi Arabia faces the possibility of an Iranian transfer of weapons of weapons of mass destruction to some anti-
Saudi extremist group or proxy. These currently do not seem to be
probable scenarios, but Saudi Arabia is worried.

Senior Saudi officials have said that Saudi Arabia has examined
its options for responding to such an Iranian threat, including an
effort to acquire its own nuclear weapons, but that it has rejected such
an option. The Saudi media has also recognized the threat. For example, an article by Abdurrahman Alrashid in the newspaper *Al-Sharq
Alawsat* stated: "Yes, we are afraid of the Iranian Uranium." He went on
to argue that "the Iranians are not building the bomb only to threaten
Israel and the United States, but also the Gulf countries. Iran has
tried to dominate the Gulf region since the revolution, and continues
to this day."[26]

POSSIBLE DATES FOR IRAN'S ACQUISITION
OF NUCLEAR WEAPONS

There is no way to estimate when Iran will get nuclear weapons or to be certain that Iran will push its nuclear programs forward to the point where it has actual weapons. In fact, there is a long history of estimates of possible dates that does little more than warn that such estimates are either extremely uncertain or have limited value.

Lieutenant General Binford Peay, the commander of USCENT-COM, stated in June, 1997, "I would predict to you that it would be some time at the turn of the next century. . . . I wouldn't want to put a date on it. I don't know if its 2010, 2007, 2003. I am just saying its coming closer. Your instincts tell you that that's the kind of speed they are moving at."[27] Robert Gates, then the director of central intelligence, testified to Congress in February 1992 that Iran was "building up its special weapons capability as part of a massive . . . effort to develop its military and defense capability."[28] In 1992 press reports by the CIA, National Intelligence Estimates on this subject indicated that the CIA estimated Iran could have a nuclear weapon by 2000. Reports coming out of Israel in January 1995 also claimed that the United States and Israel estimated that Iran could have a nuclear weapon in five years.[29]

During the same period, U.S. intelligence sources denied the reports coming out of Israel and estimated that it might take 7 to 15 years for Iran to acquire a nuclear weapon.[30] As mentioned above, John Holum testified to Congress in 1995 that Iran could have the bomb by 2003. In 1997, he testified that Iran could have the bomb by 2005–2007.[31] Although 2 years had passed in which Iran might have made substantial progress, the U.S. estimate of the earliest date at which Iran could make its own bomb slipped by 2 to 4 years.

U.S. secretary of defense William Perry stated on January 9, 1995, "We believe that Iran is trying to develop a nuclear program. We believe it will be many, many years until they achieve such a capability. There are some things they might be able to do to short-cut that time."[32] In referring to "shortcuts," Secretary Perry was concerned with the risk that Iran could obtain fissile material and weapons technology from the former Soviet Union or some other nation capable of producing fissile material.

In 1996, John M. Deutch, then the director of central intelligence, testified to Congress that "we judge that Iran is actively pursuing an indigenous nuclear weapons capability. . . . Specifically, Iran is attempting to develop the capability to produce both plutonium and highly enriched uranium. In an attempt to shorten the timeline to a weapon, Iran has launched a parallel effort to purchase fissile material, mainly from sources in the former Soviet Union." He indicated that Iran's indigenous uranium-enrichment program seemed to be focused on the development of gas centrifuges and that Iran's nuclear weapons program was still at least 8 to 10 years away from producing nuclear arms, although this time could be shortened significantly with foreign assistance.[33]

A detailed Department of Defense report on proliferation was issued in 1997. It did not comment on the timing of Iran's nuclear efforts. It did, however, draw broad conclusions about the scale of the Iranian nuclear program and how it fit into Iran's overall efforts to acquire weapons of mass destruction. What is striking about this report is that some eight years later, its conclusions still seem to broadly reflect the Defense Department's views regarding Iran's efforts to acquire both weapons of mass destruction and long-range missiles:[34]

> Iran's national objectives and strategies are shaped by its regional political aspirations, threat perceptions, and the need to preserve its Islamic government. Tehran strives to be a leader in the Islamic world and seeks to be the dominant power in the Gulf. The latter goal brings it into conflict with the United States. Tehran would like to diminish Washington's political and military influence in the region. Iran also remains hostile to the ongoing Middle East peace process and supports the use of terrorism as an element of policy. Within the framework of its national goals, Iran continues to give high priority to expanding its NBC [nuclear, biological, and chemical] weapons and missile programs. In addition, Iran's emphasis on pursuing independent production capabilities for NBC weapons and missiles is driven by its experience during the 1980–1988 war with Iraq, during which it was unable to respond adequately to Iraqi chemical and missile attacks and suffered the effects of an international arms embargo.

> Iran perceives that it is located in a volatile and dangerous region, virtually surrounded by potential military threats or unstable neighbors. These include the Iraqi government of Saddam Hussein, Israel, U.S. security agreements with the Gulf Cooperation Council (GCC) states and accompanying U.S. military presence in the Gulf, and instability in Afghanistan and the Central Asian states of the former Soviet Union.

Iran still views Baghdad as the primary regional threat to the Islamic Republic, even though Iraq suffered extensive damage during the Gulf War. Further, Iran is not convinced that Iraq's NBC programs will be adequately restrained or eliminated through continued UN sanctions or monitoring. Instead, the Iranians believe that they will face yet another challenge from their historical rival.

Tehran is concerned about strong U.S. ties with the GCC states because these states have received substantial amounts of modern Western conventional arms, which Tehran seeks but cannot acquire, and because U.S. security guarantees make these states less susceptible to Iranian pressure. While Tehran probably does not believe GCC nations have offensive designs against the Islamic Republic, it may be concerned that the United States will increase mistrust between Iran and the Arab states. It also likely fears that the sizable U.S. military presence in the region could lead to an attack against Iran. Iran may also be concerned by Israel's strategic projection capabilities and its potential to strike Iran in a variety of ways. For all these reasons, Tehran probably views NBC weapons and the ability to deliver them with missiles as decisive weapons for battlefield use, as deterrents, and as effective means for political intimidation of less powerful neighboring states.

In recent years, Iran's weak economy has limited the development of its NBC weapons and missile programs, although oil price increases in 1996 may have relieved the pressure at least temporarily. Tehran's international debt exceeds $30 billion, although Iran is meeting its debt repayment obligations. Iran also is facing a rapidly growing population that will exact greater future demands from its limited economy. Despite these internal problems, Iran assigns a high priority to attaining production self-sufficiency for NBC weapons and missiles. Therefore, funding for these efforts is likely to be a high priority for the next several years.

Tehran has attempted to portray U.S. containment efforts as unjust, in an attempt to convince European or Asian suppliers to relax export restrictions on key technologies. At the same time, foreign suppliers must consider the risk of sanctions or political embarrassment because of U.S.-led containment efforts.

Iran's nuclear program, focusing on electric power production, began during the 1970s under the Shah. Research and development efforts also were conducted on fissile material production, although these efforts were halted during the Iranian revolution and the Iran-Iraq war. However, the program has been restarted, possibly in reaction to the revelations about the scope of Iraq's nuclear weapons program.

Iran is trying to acquire fissile material to support development of nuclear weapons and has set up an elaborate system of military and civilian organizations to support its effort. Barring outright acquisition of a nuclear weapon from a foreign source, Iran could pursue several other avenues for weapon development. The shortest route, depending on weapon design, could be to purchase or steal fissile material. Also, Iran could attempt to produce highly enriched uranium if it acquired the appropriate facilities for the front-end of the nuclear fuel cycle. Finally, Iran could pursue development of an entire fuel cycle, which would allow for long-term production of plutonium, similar to the route North Korea followed.

Iran does not yet have the necessary infrastructure to support a nuclear weapons program, although is actively negotiating for purchase of technologies and whole facilities to support all of the above strategies. Iran claims it is trying to establish a complete nuclear fuel cycle to support a civilian energy program, but this same fuel cycle would be applicable to a nuclear weapons development program. Iran is seeking foreign sources for many elements of the nuclear fuel cycle. Chinese and Russian supply policies are key to whether Iran will successfully acquire the needed technology, expertise, and infrastructure to manufacture the fissile material for a weapon and the ability to fashion a usable device. Russian or Chinese supply of nuclear power reactors, allowed by the NPT, could enhance Iran's limited nuclear infrastructure and advance its nuclear weapons program.

Iran has had a chemical weapons production program since early in the Iran-Iraq war. It used chemical agents to respond to Iraqi chemical attacks on several occasions during that war. Since the early 1990s, it has put a high priority on its chemical weapons program because of its inability to respond in kind to Iraq's chemical attacks and the discovery of substantial Iraqi efforts with advanced agents, such as the highly persistent nerve agent VX. Iran ratified the CWC, under which it will be obligated to eliminate its chemical program over a period of years. Nevertheless, it continues to upgrade and expand its chemical warfare production infrastructure and munitions arsenal.

Iran manufactures weapons for blister, blood, and choking agents; it is also believed to be conducting research on nerve agents. Iran has a stockpile of these weapons, including artillery shells and bombs, which could be used in another conflict in the region.

Although Iran is making a concerted effort to attain an independent production capability for all aspects of its chemical weapons program, it remains dependent on foreign sources for chemical warfare-related technologies. China is an important supplier of technologies and equipment for Iran's chemical warfare program. Therefore, Chinese supply policies will be key to whether Tehran attains its long-term goal of independent production for these weapons.

Iran's biological warfare program began during the Iran-Iraq war. The pace of the program probably has increased because of the 1995 revelations about the scale of Iraqi efforts prior to the Gulf War. The relative low cost of developing these weapons may be another motivating factor. Although this program is in the research and development stage, the Iranians have considerable expertise with pharmaceuticals, as well as the commercial and military infrastructure needed to produce basic biological warfare agents. Iran also can make some of the hardware needed to manufacture agents. Therefore, while only small quantities of usable agent may exist now, within 10 years, Iran's military forces may be able to deliver biological agents effectively. Iran has ratified the BWC.

Iran has an ambitious missile program, with SCUD B, SCUD C, and CSS-8 (a Chinese surface-to-surface missile derived from a surface-to-air missile) missiles in its inventory. Having first acquired SCUD missiles from Libya and North Korea for use during the Iran-Iraq war, the Iranians are now able to produce the missile themselves. This has been accomplished with considerable equipment and technical help from North Korea. Iran has made significant progress in the last few years toward its goal of becoming self-sufficient in ballistic missile production.

Iran produces the solid-propellant 150 kilometer range Nazeat 10 and 200 kilometer range Zelzal unguided rockets. Iran also is trying to produce a relatively short-range solid-propellant missile. For the longer term, Iran's goal is to establish the capability to produce medium range ballistic missiles to expand its regional influence. It is attempting to acquire production infrastructure to enable it to produce the missiles itself. Like many of Iran's other efforts, success with future missile capabilities will depend on key equipment and technologies from China, North Korea, and Russia.

Iran's missiles allow it to strike a wide variety of key economic and military targets in several neighboring countries, including Turkey, Saudi Arabia, and the other Gulf states. Possible targets include oil installations, airfields, and ports, as well as U.S. military deployment areas in the region. All of Iran's missiles are on mobile launchers, which enhance their survivability. Should Iran succeed in acquiring or developing a longer range missile like the North Korean No Dong, it could threaten an even broader area, including much of Israel.

Iran has purchased land-, sea, and air-launched short range cruise missiles from China; it also has a variety of foreign-made air-launched short range tactical missiles. Many of these systems are deployed as anti-ship weapons in or near the Gulf. Iran also has a variety of Western and Soviet-made fighter aircraft, artillery, and rockets available as potential means of delivery for NBC weapons.

In the future, as Iran becomes more self-sufficient at producing chemical or biological agents and ballistic missiles, there is a potential that it will become a supplier. For example, Iran might supply related equipment and technologies to other states trying to develop capabilities, such as Libya or Syria. There is precedent for such action; Iran supplied Libya with chemical agents in 1987.

Martin Indyck, the assistant secretary of state for Near East affairs, testified to the Senate Foreign Relations Committee on July 28, 1998, that Iran's Shihab-3 and Shihab-4 programs were clearly linked to its efforts to acquire nuclear weapons. He made it clear that the missiles would give Iran the range to hit targets in Israel, Turkey, and Saudi Arabia. With regard to Iran's nuclear program, Indyck stated that Iran had a "clandestine nuclear weapons program. People tend to say that a nuclear weapons capability is many years off. Our assessments vary. I would want to be a bit cautious about that because I believe there are large gaps in our knowledge of what is going on there because it's a clandestine program."[35]

There has been relatively little new formal testimony on the nature of U.S. estimates of the timing of Iran's nuclear program, and the director of the CIA did not address this subject in his testimony to Congress on the "World Wide Threat" on February 2, 2000. U.S. intelligence has, however, continued to flag the Iranian nuclear threat as part of its broader assessments of Iran's efforts to proliferate. Since 1997, the Non-Proliferation Center of the Office of the Director of Central Intelligence has issued a series of unclassified reports on Iran's efforts to acquire nuclear weapons technology. The most recent version of the report, issued in February 2000, focuses on developments in Iran since 1998:[36]

Iran remains one of the most active countries seeking to acquire WMD and ACW [advanced conventional weapons] technology from abroad. In doing so, Tehran is attempting to develop an indigenous capability to produce various types of weapons—nuclear, chemical, and biological— and their delivery systems. During the reporting period, Iran focused its efforts to acquire WMD- and ACW- related equipment, materials, and technology primarily on entities in Russia, China, North Korea and Western Europe.

For the first half of 1999, entities in Russia and China continued to supply a considerable amount and a wide variety of ballistic missile-related goods and technology to Iran. Tehran is using these goods and technologies to support current production programs and to achieve its goal of becoming self-sufficient in the production of ballistic missiles. Iran already is producing Scud short-range ballistic missiles (SRBMs) and has built and publicly displayed prototypes for the Shahab-3 medium-range ballistic missile (MRBM), which had its initial flight test in July 1998 and probably has achieved "emergency operational capability"—i.e., Tehran could deploy a limited number of the Shahab-3 prototype missiles in an operational mode during a perceived crisis situation. In addition, Iran's Defense Minister last year publicly acknowledged the development of the Shahab-4, originally calling it a more capable ballistic missile than the Shahab-3, but later categorizing it as solely a space launch vehicle with no military applications. Iran's Defense Minister also has publicly mentioned plans for a "Shahab 5."

For the reporting period, Tehran continued to seek considerable dual-use biotechnical equipment from entities in Russia and Western Europe, ostensibly for civilian uses. Iran began a biological warfare (BW) program during the Iran-Iraq war, and it may have some limited capability for BW deployment. Outside assistance is both important and difficult to prevent, given the dual-use nature of the materials, the equipment being sought, and the many legitimate end uses for these items.

Iran, a Chemical Weapons Convention (CWC) party, already has manufactured and stockpiled chemical weapons, including blister, blood, and choking agents and the bombs and artillery shells for delivering them. During the first half of 1999, Tehran continued to seek production technology, expertise, and chemicals that could be used as precursor agents in its chemical warfare (CW) program from entities in Russia and China. It also acquired or attempted to acquire indirectly through intermediaries in other countries equipment and material that could be used to create a more advanced and self-sufficient CW infrastructure.

Iran sought nuclear-related equipment, material, and technical expertise from a variety of sources, especially in Russia, during the first half of 1999. Work continues on the construction of a 1,000-megawatt nuclear power reactor in Bushehr, Iran, that will be subject to International Atomic Energy Agency (IAEA) safeguards. In addition, Russian entities continued to interact with Iranian research centers on various activities. These projects will help Iran augment its nuclear technology infrastructure, which in turn would be useful in supporting nuclear weapons research and development. The expertise and technology gained, along with the commercial channels and contacts established-even from cooperation that appears strictly civilian in nature-could be used to advance Iran's nuclear weapons research and developmental program.

Russia has committed to observe certain limits on its nuclear cooperation with Iran. For example, President Yeltsin has stated publicly that Russia will not provide militarily useful nuclear technology to Iran. Beginning in January 1998, the Russian Government took a number of steps to increase its oversight of entities involved in dealings with Iran and other states of proliferation concern. In 1999, it pushed a new export control law through the Duma. Russian firms, however, faced economic pressures to circumvent these controls and did so in some cases. The Russian Government, moreover, failed in some cases regarding Iran to enforce its export controls. Following repeated warnings, the U.S. Government in January 1999 imposed administrative measures against Russian entities that had engaged in nuclear- and missile-related cooperation with Iran. The measures imposed on these and other Russian entities (which were identified in 1998) remain in effect.

China pledged in October 1997 not to engage in any new nuclear cooperation with Iran but said it would complete cooperation on two ongoing nuclear projects, a small research reactor and a zirconium production facility at Esfahan that Iran will use to produce cladding for reactor fuel. The pledge appears to be holding. As a party to the Nuclear Nonproliferation Treaty (NPT), Iran is required to apply IAEA safeguards to nuclear fuel, but safeguards are not required for the zirconium plant or its products.

Iran is attempting to establish a complete nuclear fuel cycle for its civilian energy program. In that guise, it seeks to obtain whole facilities, such as a uranium conversion facility, that, in fact, could be used in any number of ways in support of efforts to produce fissile material needed for a nuclear weapon. Despite international efforts to curtail the flow of critical technologies and equipment, Tehran continues to seek fissile material and technology for weapons development and has set up an elaborate system of military and civilian organizations to support its effort.

Unofficial or leaked estimates have, however, appeared to grow more pessimistic in recent years. The *New York Times* and *Washington Post* published reports in January 2000 that the CIA now estimated that it could not characterize the timing of the Iranian nuclear weapons program and that Iran might already have a bomb. These reports, however, seem to have dealt with an intelligence report that focused on the inherent uncertainties in estimating Iranian capabilities, rather than to have been the result of any radical change in an estimate of how rapidly Iran could produce a weapon.[37]

Further leaks—following the *New York Times* report—indicated that the CIA had concluded that Iran was capable of completing the design and manufacture of all aspects of a nuclear weapon except the acquisition of fissile material—an accomplishment that Iraq had also mastered by 1990. Though the details of the report were never leaked, it seems likely that it concluded that Iran could now design medium-sized plutonium and uranium weapons, and manufacture the high-explosive lens, neutron initiators, high-speed capacitors, and other components of the weapon. It could conduct fissile simulations of the explosive behavior of such designs using modern test equipment in ways similar to the Iraqi and Pakistani nuclear programs, and it could rapidly assemble a weapon from these components if it could obtain illegal fissile material.

It seems likely that the report concluded that Iran now had the technology to process highly enriched plutonium simply because no country that has ever seriously attempted such processing has failed, but Iran would need fissile or borderline fissile uranium to make a bomb. As a result, the key uncertainty was whether the United States could monitor all potential sources of fissile material with enough accuracy to ensure that Iran did not have a weapon—and the answer was no.

Although any such conclusions are speculative, it also seems likely that the U.S. intelligence community concluded that it is not possible to perfectly identify the level of Iranian nuclear weapons efforts, the specific organizations involved, the location and nature of all facilities, the foreign purchasing offices, and Iran's technical success. U.S. intelligence certainly knows far more than it makes public, but Iran has been carrying out a covert program since the shah without one known case of a major defector or public example of a reliable breakthrough in human intelligence. It also learned during the Iran-Iraq War that it needed to ensure its facilities were not centralized and vulnerable and that it had to conceal its activities as much as possible from any kind of intelligence surveillance. The strengthening of the NPT inspection regime, and Iran's search for a more moderate effort, have almost certainly reinforced these efforts to conceal its programs.[38]

The CIA's deputy director for intelligence, John McLaughlin, made the following broad comments on the uncertainties in estimating the nature of efforts to proliferate in an interview in January 2000:[39]

> I would say the problem of proliferation of weapons of mass destruction is becoming more complex and difficult. . . . We're starting to see more evidence of what I might call kind of secondary proliferation. That is more evidence of sharing of information and data among countries that are striving to obtain weapons. . . . As the systems mature in the obvious countries like North Korea and Iran, they themselves have the potential to start becoming sources of proliferation as distinct from aspirants. And that begins to complicate the whole picture. . . . In the intelligence business (denial and deception) is an art form unto itself, it is how do you deny information to the other side and how do you deceive the other side? . . . Countries that are building such weapons are learning more and more about how to do that, making our job harder. . . . So if there is an issue that is to me personally worrying, it's the increasing complexity of the proliferation challenge. . . . To some degree we're dealing with problems that are fuelled by hundreds of years of history. At the same time this past is colliding with the future, because you have these same people now using laptop computers and commercial encryption. . . . You're not going to find that information on their Web sites. You're going to have to go out and get it somewhere clandestinely, either through human collection or through technical means.

The most recent unclassified CIA report on Iran's efforts covers developments through the end of 2003 and was issued in the spring of 2004. It makes the following judgments about Iran's nuclear weapons efforts and other programs, and though these do not take account of the developments in 2004 discussed above, they still seem to broadly reflect current U.S. intelligence assessments:[40]

Iran continued to vigorously pursue indigenous programs to produce nuclear, chemical, and biological weapons. Iran is also working to improve delivery systems as well as ACW. To this end, Iran continued to seek foreign materials, training, equipment, and know-how. During the reporting period, Iran still focused particularly on entities in Russia, China, North Korea, and Europe. Iran's nuclear program received significant assistance in the past from the proliferation network headed by Pakistani scientist A.Q. Khan.

Nuclear. The United States remains convinced that Tehran has been pursuing a clandestine nuclear weapons program, in contradiction to its obligations as a party to the Nuclear Non-proliferation Treaty (NPT). During 2003, Iran continued to pursue an indigenous nuclear fuel cycle ostensibly for civilian purposes but with clear weapons potential. International scrutiny and International Atomic Energy Agency (IAEA) inspections and safeguards will most likely prevent Tehran from using facilities declared to the IAEA directly for its weapons program as long as Tehran remains a party to the NPT. However, Iran could use the same technology at other, covert locations for military applications.

Iran continues to use its civilian nuclear energy program to justify its efforts to establish domestically or otherwise acquire the entire nuclear fuel cycle. Iran claims that this fuel cycle would be used to produce fuel for nuclear power reactors, such as the 1,000-megawatt light-water reactor that Russia is continuing to build at the southern port city of Bushehr. However, Iran does not need to produce its own fuel for this reactor because Russia has pledged to provide the fuel throughout the operating lifetime of the reactor and is negotiating with Iran to take back the irradiated spent fuel. An Iranian opposition group, beginning in August of 2002, revealed several previously undisclosed Iranian nuclear facilities, sparking numerous IAEA inspections since February 2003. Subsequent reports by the IAEA Director General revealed numerous failures by Iran to disclose facilities and activities, which run contrary to its IAEA safeguards obligations. Before the reporting period, the A. Q. Khan network provided Iran with designs for Pakistan's older centrifuges, as well as designs for more advanced and efficient models, and components.

The November 2003 report of the IAEA Director General (DG) to the Board of Governors describes a pattern of Iranian safeguards breaches, including the failure to: report the import and chemical conversion of uranium compounds, report the separation of plutonium from irradiated uranium targets, report the enrichment of uranium using both centrifuges and lasers, and provide design information for numerous fuel cycle facilities. In October 2003, Iran sent a report to the DG providing additional detail on its nuclear program and signed an agreement with the United Kingdom, France, and Germany that included an Iranian promise to suspend all enrichment and reprocessing efforts. On 18 December 2003, Iran signed the Additional Protocol (AP) to its IAEA Safeguards Agreement but took no steps to ratify the Protocol during this reporting period.

Ballistic Missile. Ballistic missile-related cooperation from entities in the former Soviet Union, North Korea, and China over the years has helped Iran move toward its goal of becoming self-sufficient in the production of ballistic missiles. Such assistance during 2003 continued to include equipment, technology, and expertise. Iran's ballistic missile inventory is among the largest in the Middle East and includes some 1,300-km-range Shahab-3 medium-range ballistic missiles (MRBMs) and a few hundred short-range ballistic missiles (SRBMs)-including the Shahab-1 (Scud-B), Shahab-2 (Scud C), and Tondar-69 (CSS-8)-as well as a variety of large unguided rockets. Already producing Scud SRBMs, Iran announced that it had begun production of the Shahab-3 MRBM and a new solid-propellant SRBM, the Fateh-110. In addition, Iran publicly acknowledged the development of follow-on versions of the Shahab-3. It originally said that another version, the Shahab-4, was a more capable ballistic missile than its predecessor but later characterized it as solely a space launch vehicle with no military applications. Iran is also pursuing longer-range ballistic missiles.

Chemical. Iran is a party to the Chemical Weapons Convention (CWC). Nevertheless, during the reporting period it continued to seek production technology, training, and expertise from foreign entities that could further Tehran's efforts to achieve an indigenous capability to produce nerve agents. Iran may have already stockpiled blister, blood, choking, and possibly nerve agents-and the bombs and artillery shells to deliver them-which it previously had manufactured.

Biological. Even though Iran is part of the Biological Weapons Convention (BWC), Tehran probably maintained an offensive BW program. Iran continued to seek dual-use biotechnical materials, equipment, and expertise that could be used in Tehran's BW program. Iran probably has the capability to produce at least small quantities of BW agents.

Advanced Conventional Weapons. Iran continued to seek and acquire conventional weapons and production technologies, primarily from Russia, China, and North Korea. Tehran also sought high-quality products, particularly weapons components and dual-use items, or products that proved difficult to acquire through normal governmental channels.

Major General Aharon Zeevi Farkash, the head of Israeli Military Intelligence, stated in August 2004 that "once they have the ability to produce enough enriched Uranium, we estimate that the first bomb will be constructed within two years—i.e., the end of 2006 or the beginning of 2007."[41]

At present, most experts feel that Iran has all the basic technology to build a bomb but lacks any rapid route to getting fissile uranium and plutonium unless it can steal or buy it from another country. They also believe that Iran is increasingly worried about preemptive strikes by Israel or the United States. As a result, some feel that Iran has deliberately has lowered the profile of its activities and only conducts a low-to-moderate-level weapons design and development effort.[42] As a result, many feel that Iran is at least to five to seven years away from acquiring a nuclear device using its own enriched material, and six to nine years away from acquiring the ability to design a nuclear weapon that can be fitted in the warhead of a long-range missile system.

There are experts, however, who feel that Iran is working actively on the design of missile warheads and bombs at a level of activity indicating that it may well be significantly closer to having a bomb. These experts also feel that Iran has a covert nuclear weapons design and enrichment effort that has developed in parallel with its more overt nuclear research and power activities, and that the elements of this program are well dispersed and are designed to have denial covers that can claim they are peaceful research or efforts conducted in the past. They state that the information they rely on has not been provided by opposition sources.[43]

Much hinges on the level of centrifuge development that Iran has achieved and its covert ability to acquire or manufacture centrifuges and to assemble them into chains that can be hidden and deployed either in large underground/sheltered facilities or in buildings that appear to have other uses. Experts disagree over Iran's level of technology, which can make the difference between chains of hundreds and thousands of centrifuges, and whether it has moved beyond the limited levels of efficiency found in the P-2 centrifuges being manufactured for Libya. Rotor design and overall efficiency are critical in determining the size of the facilities needed to spin uranium hexaflouride into enriched uranium, and how quickly Iran could acquire a weapon. There are significant time gaps and uncertainties in the data Iran has provided to the IAEA, and it may have advanced beyond the designs of the 20 centrifuges it has declared to the IAEA. This is, however, a major wild card in estimating Iran's progress.[44]

Another wild card in these estimates is that the deadlines would change radically if Iran could buy fissile material from another nation or source—such as the 500 kilograms of fissile material the United States airlifted out of Kazakhstan in 1994. This was enough material to make up to 25 nuclear weapons, and the United States acted primarily because Iran was actively seeking to buy such material.[45] If Iran could obtain weapons grade material, a number of experts believe that it could probably develop a gun or simple implosion nuclear weapon in 9 to 36 months and might be able to deploy an implosion weapon suited for missile warhead or bomb delivery in the same period.

The risk of such a transfer of fissile material is significant. U.S. experts believe that all the weapons and fissile material remaining in the former Soviet Union are now stored in Russian facilities. The security of these facilities is still erratic, however, and there is a black market in nuclear material. Though the radioactive material sold on the black market by the Commonwealth of Independent States and Central European citizens to date has consisted largely of plutonium-240, low-grade enriched uranium, or isotopes of material that have little value in a nuclear weapons program, this is no guarantee for the future. There are also no guarantees that Iran will not be able to purchase major transfers of nuclear weapons components and nuclear ballistic missile warhead technology.

IRAN'S NUCLEAR WAR-FIGHTING DOCTRINE AND CAPABILITIES

Few meaningful data are available on Iranian nuclear doctrine and targeting—to the extent current plans would even be relevant in the future. The same is true of Iranian plans to limit the vulnerability of its weapons and facilities—and whether Iran would try to create a launch-on-warning or launch-under-attack capability. It is easy to speculate at vast length on what Iran would do with nuclear weapons. However, it is impossible to determine how aggressively Iran would exploit such a capability in threatening or intimidating its neighbors, or putting pressure on the West. Attempts to guess at Iran's war-fighting doctrine and actions in using weapons of mass destruction simply lack meaningful data.

It is also quite possible that Iran has not yet looked far enough beyond its nuclear weapons acquisition efforts to work out detailed plans for possession. There is no way to know if Iran would choose a relatively stable model of deterrence or aggressively exploit its possession politically. It is equally difficult to guess whether Iran would develop an aggressive doctrine for use, consider developing a launch-on-warning or launch-under-attack capability, or reserve the use of such a weapon for a last resort.[46]

As for war-fighting capability, any working nuclear device that Iran is likely to develop will be sufficient to destroy any hardened target, area target, or city in the Middle East if the delivery vehicle is accurate enough. Nuclear weapons do, however, differ sharply in their effect as they grow in size; and if Iran had to rely on inaccurate delivery systems, it not only would have to aim at area targets like cities and major energy facilities but also might have to either use multiple strikes or develop more advanced and higher-yield nuclear matériel like "boosted weapons." Alternatively, it might rely on ground bursts and fallout.

Iran's nuclear efforts will also interact heavily with the progress it makes in biological and chemical weapons programs and its efforts to improve its delivery capabilities. By the time Iran has significant nuclear capability, it may have significant missile, cruise missile, and long-range strike aircraft capability—although it may not have cruise missiles capable of carrying a nuclear weapon. It may also have rebuilt much of its conventional capability to the point where it has significant war-fighting capabilities.

Regardless of which weapons of mass destruction Iran develops and deploys, it will encounter certain practical problems:

- Unless Iran acquires satellites, it will have limited dynamic targeting capability and limited ability to assess the impact of any strikes it launches. Even if it does acquire satellites, it will experience serious problems in trying to assess damage and its target and escalatory options in the event of a chemical and biological strike or in terms of nuclear fallout.

- It would take a major surface testing effort to be certain of the reliability and yield of its weapons designs, and testing of actual bombs and warheads to know the success of its weaponization effort—although a nuclear devise could be tested using noncritical materials to determine that its explosive and triggering systems functioned.

- Quite aside from theoretical accuracy problems, long-range missiles are subject to some loss of accuracy depending on the vector they are fired in, as well as potential weather effects. Combined with targeting, weapons design, and other accuracy problems—plus reliability problems—a significant number of Iranian strikes might miss their targets and some might hit unintended targets.

- Past tests have shown that efforts to apply chemical and biological lethality data based on laboratory or limited human testing simply do not provide anything approaching an accurate picture of area lethality. Nominal lethality data can be wrong by more than an order of magnitude—so far, by exaggerating lethality. The impact of nuclear strikes on large, semihard area targets is very hard to predict. So is the effect of unusual winds and weather.

- Iranian C^4I systems might not be adequate and survivable enough to maintain cohesive control over Iran weapons and launch forces. Any reliance on launch on warning or launch under attack virtually precludes such control, and it could trigger Iranian action based on false alarms or a serious misunderstanding of the developing tactical situation. If Iran were preempted or subject to a first strike, its ability to characterize the result could be equally uncertain.

- Iran might well have equal problems in characterizing enemy responses and retaliatory strikes once exchanges began.

- For all these reasons, Iranian command and control might well have to operate on the basis of grossly inadequate information in both planning operations and conducting them. The "fog of war" might well be exceptionally dense.

What is clear is that if Iran acquired a working nuclear device, this would suddenly and radically change perceptions of the military balance in the region. Iran is likely to acquire such weapons at about the same time it acquires MRBMs, and this would be a volatile combination. Iran could then destroy any hardened target, area target, or city within the range of its delivery systems. Iran's Southern Gulf neighbors are extremely vulnerable to attacks on a few cities, and even one successful nuclear attack might force a fundamental restructuring of their politics and/or economy. They are effectively "one-bomb" countries. The same is true of Israel, although it has limited missile defenses and is steadily improving them and could launch a massive retaliatory nuclear armed missile strike against virtually all of Iran's cities.

Iranian nuclear capabilities would raise major medium-term and long-term challenges to Saudi Arabia, the other Southern Gulf states, Iraq, Israel, and the West in deterrence, defense, retaliation, and arms control. Iran can almost certainly continue to disguise most of the necessary R&D effort to go on developing improved enrichment and weapons design and manufacture technology regardless of the limits placed upon it by IAEA inspections and its agreements with Europe. These could include the ballistic testing of weapons and warheads with the same weight, size, and balance as real weapons, and the use of complex simulation and testing with nuclear weapons designs that are workable in every respect except that they substitute material with lower levels of enrichment for Pu-239 or highly enriched uranium.

There is the possibility that Iran's efforts could lead to U.S. and Israeli preemption against Iran's developing nuclear weapons production facilities if either country felt confident that it could destroy them with conventional weapons—and that there was an urgent need to do so. This, however, presents serious problems for the United States and Israel. Iran has extensive numbers of known nuclear facilities and is a large country that could conceal many more.

Even if a preemptive strike were initially successful, Iran could continue its efforts by placing them in many dispersed small and redundant facilities, and/or putting them deep underground. Even P-2 centrifuge enrichment facilities can be deployed in small chains that can be "folded" to fit in virtually any building, and made redundant by having multiple small chains and moving steadily more enriched material from one building to another.

Iran can proceed to deploy its Shahab missiles as conventionally armed missiles, and it can give them mobility to hide them or organize them with suitable warning and command-and-control system so they can launch on warning or launch under attack. It can "instantly" convert part of its air force to a launch-on-warning or launch-under-attack capability simply by arming them with nuclear weapons and putting them on alert. Even a few nuclear deployments of this kind could act as a powerful deterrent to both Israel and the United States and could seriously damage any Gulf state or major Gulf energy facility.

Saudi Arabia and its neighbors can respond with accelerated efforts to deploy theater missile defenses—although such systems seem more likely to be "confidence builders" than leakproof. It would almost certainly lead the United States to consider counterproliferation strikes on Iran and to work with its Southern Gulf allies in developing an adequate deterrent. Given the U.S. rejection of biological and chemical weapons, this raises the possibility of creating a major U.S. theater nuclear deterrent, although such a deterrent could be sea and air based and deployed outside the Gulf. If the United States failed to provide such a deterrent and /or missile defenses, it seems likely that the Southern Gulf states would be forced to accommodate Iran or seek weapons of mass destruction of their own.

Notes

[1] *Washington Post,* November 18, 2004.

[2] Shirley Kan, "China's Proliferation of Weapons of Mass Destruction," Congressional Research Service, CRS IB 9256, March 1, 2002.

[3] Merav Zafary, "Iranian Biological and Chemical Weapons Profile Study," Center for Nonproliferation Studies, Monterey Institute of International Studies, February 2001.

[4] *Jane's Sentinel Security Assessment: The Gulf States,* "Iran," October 7, 2004.

[5] The following list summarizes the far more comprehensive descriptions of Iranian nuclear facilities developed by GlobalSecurity.org, headed by John Pike. The full analysis for Iranian facilities can be found at the GlobalSecurity.org Web site, Iran Nuclear Facilities, http://www.globalsecurity.org/wmd/world/iran/nuke-fac.htm.

[6] All IAEA quotes are taken from the IAEA, "Implementation of the NPT Safeguards Agreement in the Islamic Republic of Iran," Report by the Director General to the Board of Governors, GOV 2004/83, November 15, 2004.

[7] IAEA, "Implementation of the NPT Safeguards Agreement in the Islamic Republic of Iran."

[8] Quoting John Bolton's testimony of June 24, 2004, to the U.S. House of Representatives Committee on International Relations, GlobalSecurity.org notes

that "according to Paul Leventhal of the Nuclear Control Institute, if Iran were to withdraw from the Nonproliferation Treaty and renounce the agreement with Russia, the Bushehr reactor could produce a quarter ton of plutonium per year, which Leventhal says is enough for at least 30 atomic bombs. Normally for electrical power production the uranium fuel remains in the reactor for three to four years, which produces a plutonium of 60 percent or less Pu-239, 25 percent or more Pu-240, 10 percent or more Pu-241, and a few percent Pu-242. The Pu-240 has a high spontaneous rate of fission, and the amount of Pu-240 in weapons-grade plutonium generally does not exceed 6 percent, with the remaining 93 percent Pu-239. Higher concentrations of Pu-240 can result in pre-detonation of the weapon, significantly reducing yield and reliability. For the production of weapons-grade plutonium with lower Pu-240 concentrations, the fuel rods in a reactor have to be changed frequently, about every four months or less."

[9] IAEA, "Implementation of the NPT Safeguards Agreement in the Islamic Republic of Iran."

[10] *Saudi Gazette*, December 6, 2004; *Arab News*, December 6, 2004; *International Herald Tribune*, December 3, 2004; *Daily Star*, December 3, 2004.

[11] IAEA, "Implementation of the NPT Safeguards Agreement in the Islamic Republic of Iran."

[12] *Saudi Gazette*, December 6, 2004; *Arab News*, December 6, 2004; *International Herald Tribune*, December 3, 2004; *Daily Star*, December 3, 2004.

[13] IAEA, "Implementation of the NPT Safeguards Agreement in the Islamic Republic of Iran."

[14] Ibid.

[15] "Iran Declaration," http://news.bbc.co.uk/1/hiworld/middle_east/3211036; International Crisis Group, "Iran: Where Next on the Nuclear Standoff," *Middle East Briefing*, Amman/Brussels, November 24, 2004, 2–3.

[16] *Guardian*, June 28, 2004.

[17] International Crisis Group, "Iran," 15; *Jane's Intelligence Review*, August 19, 2004; UPI, August 9, 2004.

[18] Sanger, "Pakistan Found to Aid Iran Nuclear Efforts."

[19] "Text of EU–Iran Nuclear Agreement," *Albawaba*.

[20] *New York Times*, November 23, 2004; International Crisis Group, "Iran," 4–7.

[21] Jahn, "Iran Satisfies IAEA."

[22] Dareini, "Iran Suspends Uranium Enrichment."

[23] IAEA, "Implementation of the NPT Safeguards Agreement in the Islamic Republic of Iran."

[24] Robin Wright and Keith Richburg, "Powell Says Iran Is Pursuing Bomb," *Washington Post*, November 18, 2004.

[25] Bill Gertz, "US Told of Iranian Effort to Create Nuclear Warhead," *Washington Times*, December 2, 2004.

[26] Abdulrahman Alrashid, "Yes We Are Afraid of the Iranian Uranium," *Al-Sharq Al-Awsat*, October 8, 2003.

[27] Speech at the annual USCENTCOM conference, June 26, 1997.

[28] *Los Angeles Times*, March 17, 1992.

[29] *New York Times*, November 30, 1992, and January 5, 1995; *Washington Times*, January 6, 1995.

[30] *New York Times*, January 10, 1995; *Jane's Intelligence Review*, "Iran's Weapons of Mass Destruction," Special Report 6, May 1995, 4–14; Gerald White, *Risk Report* 1, no. 7 (September, 1995); *Jane's Intelligence Review*, October 1995, 452.

[31] Associated Press, May 5, 1997.

[32] *Chalk Times*, January 10, 1995; *Washington Times*, January 19, 1995.

[33] Rodney W. Jones and Mark G. McDonough with Toby Dalton and Gregory Koblentz, *Tracking Nuclear Proliferation: A Guide in Maps and Charts, 1998* (Washington, D.C.: Carnegie Endowment for International Peace, 1999).

[34] The text of the report is available at http://www.defenselink.mil/pubs/prolif97/graphics.html.

[35] *Washington Times*, July 29, 1998.

[36] Non-Proliferation Center, Office of the Director of Central Intelligence, "Unclassified Report to Congress on the Acquisition of Technology Relating to Weapons of Mass Destruction and Advanced Conventional Munitions 1 January through 30 June 1999." This report was issued in response to a congressionally directed action in Section 721 of the fiscal year 1997 Intelligence Authorization Act, which requires: "(a) Not later than 6 months after the date of the enactment of this Act, and every 6 months thereafter, the Director of Central Intelligence [DCI] shall submit to Congress a report on (1) the acquisition by foreign countries during the preceding 6 months of dual-use and other technology useful for the development or production of weapons of mass destruction (including nuclear weapons, chemical weapons, and biological weapons) and advanced conventional munitions; and (2) trends in the acquisition of such technology by such countries." At the DCI's request, the DCI Nonproliferation Center (NPC) drafts this report and coordinates it throughout the intelligence community. As directed by Section 721, subsection (b), of the act, it is unclassified. As such, the report does not present the details of the intelligence community's assessments of weapons of mass destruction and advanced conventional munitions programs that are available in other classified reports and briefings for Congress.

[37] *New York Times*, January 17, 2000; Bloomberg News, January 17, 2000; Reuters, January 17, 2000; Associated Press, January 18, 2000.

[38] Reuters, January 24 and 26, 2000.

[39] Reuters, January 24, 2000.

[40] Office of the Director of Central Intelligence, CIA, "Unclassified Report to Congress on the Acquisition of Technology Relating to Weapons of Mass Destruction and Advanced Conventional Munitions, 1 July through 31 December 2003," http://www.cia.gov/cia/reports/721_reports/july_dec2003.htm.

[41] *Jane's Intelligence Review*, August 19, 2004; International Crisis Group, "Iran," 15.

[42] *Washington Times*, May 17, 1995; Office of the Secretary of Defense, *Proliferation: Threat and Response* (Washington, D.C.: U.S. Department of Defense, 1996), 12–16.

[43] Bill Gertz, "US Told of Iranian Effort to Create Nuclear Warhead," *Washington Times*, December 2, 2004; Douglas Jehl, "Iran Is Said to Work on New Missile," *International Herald Tribune*, December 2, 2004; Douglas Jehl, "Iran Reportedly Hides Work on a Long-Range Missile, *New York Times*, December 2, 2004.

[44] Most experts feel Iran has not made significant progress in any covert reactor program large enough to produce weapons materials, or in LIS.

[45] *New York Times*, May 14, 1995; *Washington Post*, November 5, 1997.

[46] For interesting insights into possible scenarios and their implications, see Anthony H. Cordesman, "Terrorism and the Threat from Weapons of Mass Destruction in the Middle East: The Problem of Paradigm Shift," CSIS, Washington, October 17, 1996; Brad Roberts, *Terrorism with Chemical and Biological Weapons, Calibrating Risks and Responses* (Alexandria: Chemical and Biological Weapons Control Institute, 1997); Shai Feldman, *Nuclear Weapons and Arms Control in the Middle East* (Cambridge, Mass.: MIT Press, 1997).

ABOUT THE AUTHOR

Anthony H. Cordesman holds the Arleigh A. Burke Chair in Strategy at CSIS. He is also a national security analyst for ABC News and a frequent commentator on National Public Radio and the BBC. His television commentary has been prominently featured during the Iraq War, the conflict in Kosovo, the fighting in Afghanistan, and the Gulf War.

Prior to CSIS, Cordesman served in numerous government positions, including as national security assistant to Senator John McCain of the Senate Armed Services Committee, as director of intelligence assessment in the Office of the Secretary of Defense, as civilian assistant to the deputy secretary of defense, and as director of policy and planning for resource applications at the Department of Energy. He has also served in the State Department and on NATO International Staff and has had many foreign assignments, including posts in Lebanon, Egypt, and Iran, with extensive work in Saudi Arabia and the Gulf.

Cordesman is the author of more than 30 books on U.S. security policy, energy policy, and the Middle East, as well as a four-volume series on the lessons of modern war. His most recent books include *The War after the War: Strategic Lessons of Iraq and Afghanistan* (CSIS, 2004); *The Military Balance in the Middle East* (Praeger/CSIS, 2004); *Energy Developments in the Middle East* (Praeger/CSIS, 2004); *The Iraq War: Strategy, Tactics, and Military Lessons* (CSIS, 2003); *Saudi Arabia Enters the 21st Century* (Praeger/CSIS, 2003); *The Lessons of Afghanistan: War Fighting, Intelligence, and Force Transformation* (CSIS, 2002); and *Terrorism, Asymmetric Warfare, and Weapons of Mass Destruction* (Praeger/CSIS, 2002).